A Child in Exile

Book 3

Chapters

Forward...1

1. A Child in Exile................................2
2. The Cold War Comes Home.......................22
3. The Struggle to Regain Cuba...................37
4. The Missile Crisis............................67
5. The Rise of the Mambise Commandos.............79
6. The "Rafael Plan"............................100
7. A Global Shift of Consciousness..............125
8. A Temporary Change in Course.................142

Forward

 While reading Alejandro's account of Cuban history and the interactions of his family, I realized that this is truly a story that is common to all Cubans today. His Great-great-grandfather and mine were contemporaries in the struggle for independence from Spain as we all did our part to form our new republic. Now as Cuban-American friends in the twenty-first century, he and I similarly continue to hold true to that decade's old desire for liberty and freedom for our homeland. All Cubans can find common ground in the understanding of events that followed our independence from Spain through the rise of Castro's revolution, and many Cubans in exile today continue to hold on to the hope of one day returning home.

 "In the Company of Angels and Children", the "Whispers of Our Fathers" and the follow-on book, "A Child in Exile," are a "must read" for all young Cuban-Americans who wish to intimately connect with their history and heritage and who long to understand the struggles and sacrifices of their fellow countrymen as they fought for their right to live free.

Liliana de Céspedes
Great-great-granddaughter of
Carlos Manuel de Céspedes,
Founder of the Cuban Republic

Chapter One

A Child in Exile

"A philosopher dreamed he was a butterfly. The dream had been so vivid that when he awoke he did not know whether he was a man who had dreamed he was a butterfly fluttering among the flowers, or whether he was a butterfly who was now dreaming that he was a man."

It was October the 20th, 1960, the day my father Eduardo Carlos De La Cruz decided to move the family away to a place where the darkness was finally visible. The turmoil and violence of the Cuban Revolution had denied us a future promised by history. We were to begin again in a new and unknown land. One year and ten months earlier, the rebel army of Fidel Castro had defeated the forces of the Cuban strongman Fulgencio Batista. As a family, we found ourselves picking up the pieces in an attempt to create an image of that puzzle that was our life where we could find safety and peace.

Generations of *De La Cruz* throughout history had experienced exiles and conquest, wars and turmoil. We had been in Spain, under Muslim occupation, in Jerusalem, in Constantinople, in Cuba and now the United States. Historically, these dramatic changes in the patterns of our

lives were oddly welcomed by the family. The knowledge and experience gained by these challenges had solidified our core, that genetic code that had been passed along to generations of the family over time making our soul stronger.

Cuba in 1959 and 1960 had been full of promise and disappointment. Fidel Castro had been seen by many throughout the island as a heroic *robin-hood* figure that would liberate the nation from what had seemed a brutal dictatorship. Yet for the Cuban people, Fidel had proven to be a myth, a sort of legend and hope, but never quite the expected reality. The promise of Fidel and his revolution quickly gave way to a feeling of betrayal that many Cubans to this day are still attempting to reconcile.

The circumstances of our departure were tense to say the least. My father Eduardo De La Cruz had recently submitted his resignation as the revolutionary government's Cuban Ambassador to the Central American nation of Guatemala, and the government of Fidel Castro was on the hunt for his arrest as an enemy of the state.[1] As Castro's first Ambassador to attempt to defect to the United States, the revolutionaries had decided to make an example of him as it had done with countless other families as the revolution's power base took hold.

---

[1] Interview with Cuban Ambassador Eduardo C. delaCruz

We stood in line at the airport gate on the afternoon of our defection waiting for what seemed like days. Our flight on Pan-American World Airways was supposed to depart at 5:00 p.m., but it was announced there would be a delay to 10:00 that evening. The wait itself became a form of slow torture. While we stood in line, Castro's militia troops would frequently march in quick-step, approaching some poor soul only to drag him away to an unknown fate. We never knew when it would be our turn.

Fortunately for us, the warrant for Eduardo's arrest had not yet reached the airport authorities. My father, along with a friend, had earlier convinced the authorities at the airport that he was a member of the state security by showing them an old badge given to him by his father when he was Minister of Justice. It was a flash of false credentials done in a successful attempt to see "the list," those Cuban citizens who were being sought for arrest and who had to be prevented from leaving the island at any cost. Luckily, his name was not on the dreaded list, and for a while at least, we were safe.

The images of that October afternoon are still clear in my mind. Chaos and fear dominated the oversized crowd of middle and upper class members of Cuban society muddling about as they desperately sought to leave the island. Members of the De La Cruz family huddled together in the terminal. As

a family, we labored to become as small and invisible as possible, to simply become part of the multitude of people at the terminal that day, hidden by the fog of chaos and confusion that engulfed the Jose Marti airport terminal. This was a cruel mind game. Castro's militias were masters at creating open spaces of pain, stripping away all sense of self awareness. Common among the unlucky victims was a denial of self, a need to convince the troops that they were not the person they were seeking; that a mistake had been made. What my father was witnessing was the despair and fear elevated to heights that would cause human beings to deny their sense of existence. What does it take for a human being to hollow himself out and become devoid of all the self-identity he has spent a lifetime developing within? It was a desperate effort to disappear, to become part of the wall, the pillar, the luggage, anything but who you were.

  I was all but four years of age, yet hold on to memories of that October day. I remember the morning of our defection when my father was not with us at our home. A knock came to the door of our 8th floor apartment that overlooked the Caribbean Sea of Havana's Río Mar district. The impatient visitor did not wait for the door to be answered, and with an entitled determination, proceeded to kick down the front entrance to our home. Castro's G-2 agents and

militia troops in olive green fatigues stormed throughout the apartment attempting to serve an arrest warrant for my father. It had been pure luck that he had not been home at that time. My mother quickly went to a far off room where there was a phone with a separate line that bypassed the switchboard being monitored on the ground floor. Desperately but quietly, she made contact with him and told him to disappear, to go underground. The dark forces of this revolution were momentarily focused on us, she told him, and nothing good could come of it.

Mother and Father quickly made plans to meet at the airport for a flight to Miami. If he couldn't make it, my father advised her, she and the kids should go on without him. Clearly, there would be no chance my mother would exile to the United States with two small children alone. They would either leave their homeland together or face the consequences of remaining in Cuba together. Regardless, with luck and the determination of friends who took enormous risks to their own personal security, we closed the door to our home, turned our backs to all our personal possessions, and never returned.

The family's defection was helped by several people in and out of the Castro government, but the most important assistance was given to us by a man named Luis Buch. Mr. Buch was a prominent Cuban attorney who for years had been

the chief legal advisor to my mother's father; my grandfather Rafael Martinez Púpo. He held legal advisory control for all of grandfather's multiple business enterprises. In addition, there existed a strong bond of trust between my mother's side of the family, the Martinez clan, and the Buch family. When my mother was a pre-teen at an exclusive boarding school in Havana, she would spend all her free weekends at the Buch family estate, an expansive piece of property that was only a few doors down from the estate of the Cuban dictator Batista. She was like a daughter to Luis, and when she stayed with them over the weekend, they would frequently visit the Batista home next door.

Luis had also been a member of the Civic Resistance Movement[2] which had acted as liaison with the opposition and Castro's revolutionaries as well as with various American officials in both Cuba and the United States. He would become a trusted advisor and negotiator for Fidel Castro's insurrection. In all honesty, the family had not realized the extent of Luis's involvement with the revolution until after Castro assumed power. Part of his underground responsibilities had been to go on various international missions to discuss support for Fidel and his band in the Sierra

---

[2] Inside the Cuban Revolution: Fidel Castro and the Urban Underground
By Julia Sweig,

Maestra as far back as 1957, the year I was born. At one point he had flown to Caracas, Venezuela with the Castro portfolio, and held high level meetings to secure support in various Latin American countries for Castro's cause. He would communicate with the Castro rebels in the mountains via radio transmission, using a Morse code system that he and Che Guevara had developed, a system that only they understood.

Luis M. Buch, Fidel Castro's Minister of the Presidency

Once in power, Castro would appoint Luis Buch to the position of "Minister of the Presidency," a government position analogous to an American presidential "Chief of Staff." It was in this capacity that Luis originally recommended and insisted on the appointment of my father as Ambassador for the Revolutionary government of Cuba to the nation of Guatemala. With Castro now in power, this family

friend was now helping us to defect to the United States in an effort to save our lives.

When Castro's militia was satisfied that my father was not present at our home, they began to shadow the family on the assumption that we would eventually lead them to where Eduardo was hiding. In effect, we all waited to see which side would make the first move. Early that same afternoon, a black limousine slowly made its way to the building where we lived. The driver informed the agents that we had been summoned by the Minister of the Presidency to the Presidential Palace. A check of the license plate identified the limousine as one belonging to Luis Buch, confirming the driver's assertions and allowing the vehicle to depart without being tailed by Castro's agents. An hour later, after the agents had departed, another vehicle arrived at our Río Mar building with instructions to take our thirteen pieces of luggage to the airport.

Luckily, our luggage had been taken downstairs to a storage area in the lobby. Word had spread throughout the complex the day before our defection that the electricity would be cut off. We made haste to use the elevators when we could to bring our travel possessions down from the eighth floor. Had the militia seen our travel luggage when they served the warrant, they would have become aware of our plans to flee.

Thirteen pieces of luggage was considered by my mother to be adequate supplies for a short trip. Both my parents had planned for a two-week trip to Miami, as they were convinced beyond a doubt that the U.S. Marines would be landing to dissolve this government. The new revolutionary government had nationalized over two billion dollars in American property on the island and Marines had historically landed for much less offense. We had packed thirteen suitcases with our clothing, but nothing of great value. All our valuables had been left behind at the apartment by the simple act of closing our front door behind us. We even left the family dog behind in the care of the servants. Generations of jewels, silver and items of personal and historical significance to the family remained behind under the care of the servants that had stayed behind that day. The state militia would eventually gather all the treasure from all the abandoned mansions in Havana, systematically collecting everyone's dreams to be auctioned off in Canada.

As a family, however, we held on to the truth that what we left behind really remained unimportant, except the dog of course; we held no attachment to anything but each other. Trinkets of jewels or silver would only attract attention and create more worries for what we were about to do, placing us in greater danger. And besides, we were convinced at the time

that this journey would not be permanent and we would soon be returning home

The announcement that we were to be driven to the Presidential Palace to see Mr. Bush was a ruse of course. It had served its purpose of getting G-2 agents off our backs. Luis had gotten word of the warrant for Eduardo's arrest and correctly assumed that we would be on our way to defect to the United States. He was, after all, the only remaining moderate in the Castro government and a loyal friend. At great personal risk, he ordered the limousine to pick us up at our home and deliver us quickly and safely to the airport. In effect, we defected in style with the aid of the very government that was hunting us down.

We met clandestinely with my father at the airport and as the plane departed, the passengers held their collective breath. It wasn't until the Captain announced over the intercom that the aircraft was beyond Cuban airspace that thunderous relief and jubilation erupted in the cabin as all the passengers broke out in applause. We were finally free.

Castro's government called us "Gusanos," a Spanish word meaning "worms." That was his way of attempting to make anyone who did not believe the way he did feel like a non-human; dirt-consuming creatures. But that insult was easy to dismiss. We all knew who and what we were, and we were

secure in the knowledge that God and truth had to be on our side. We had done nothing wrong other than to have worked hard and build something that had been coveted by an illegitimate government who now simply stole everything in the name of "the people", a people who never really benefited from this theft anyway.

      Finding myself now in the United States was a strange reality for a boy of four. I was a child refugee in Florida; I laughed and played and went about my life business attempting to learn a new language and make new friends. But I was consciously frozen in the insecurity and fear that engulfed me and prevented me from finding real safety in any other place other than my bed. My evenings were a simultaneous source of security and terror. I would lay completely covered with thick blankets in the ninety degree humidity of Florida, and I would pretend that the thick blanket was an impregnable shield, a magic shield that would protect me from everything evil that was constantly knocking at my door. There were no olive green fatigues on the other side of my blanket, but they could come at any moment without any warning and it was no surprise that I wet my bed every night until I was eleven. There was nothing I could do but plow through this period of my life and attempt to make some sense

of it all. No matter what I did, I could not shake this most peculiar outcome of my evening.

Now in South Florida, there were other barriers to overcome. I remember going to our next door neighbor's home and asking the lady of the house if my new friend Wayne could come out and play. I would, of course, ask her in Spanish, but despite the language barrier, she knew why I was there. She told me that Wayne was asleep, a word that puzzled and confused me. Both my sister Lizbeth and I looked at each other in an attempt to understand "asleep." Seeing our perplexed expressions, Wayne's mother gestured with her hands held against her cheeks to show me visually what asleep meant. "I understand," I said to Liz in Spanish, "Wayne *esta durmiendo*". And so I began to learn English one word at time.

The experience of exile also led to other odd manifestations. While I could not fully comprehend the tension, I was not entirely immune to the impact of witnessing and feeling the effects on my parents and on the extended family. I began to experience some rather strange dreams growing up in Florida; some of them would remain with me as recurring dreams. While they were never a source of fear, I nevertheless couldn't shake them. In fact, I was very much intrigued by the nightly experience, always wondering if tonight would be the night that the dream would continue towards some logical conclusion that would give it some meaning. I understood even at that young age that they came from a place deeper inside me than mere consciousness. They were more like memories that told me a story or attempted to answer some question. I say this not in an attempt to reveal a certain level of personal insanity, but to demonstrate a little about the struggles and curiosities of my youth. There were variables in my life that molded and guided me, giving me the view of the world that I hold today. Some of the non-recurring dreams were more like night travels that took me to places where I would converse with various people. Strangers would briefly delay their journey to speak with me. I would ask questions and focus intensely on their stories. It was a fascinating and pleasant experience for a child now six.

   One example of such dreams led me to a field of tall grass that rose to the level just below my knees. I could gaze at my bare feet as they made their way through the tall grass. The waves of grass were visible in the rolling fields as far as my eye could see, dancing submissive to the wind. I was aware of time and knew that I was moving at a sprint, yet despite that knowledge, my feet, the grass and the wind traveled in a kind of slow motion that made me acutely aware of each step. Everything was a precise and deliberate act. My

heart pounded an almost deafening thump in my ears interrupted only by my heavy breathing. I felt nothing, no exhaustion, no strain, no sweat. All I could feel was the cool grass on my feet and an intense curiosity for my urgency. I made my way up the hill where a single tree had long ago laid claim to the land. At the base of this tree, face down; lay a dead soldier, an ancient soldier. Dressed in a white tunic, armor scattered about and leather sandals tied up to his ankles, the corpse had a gaping wound on the left side of his lower back as if pierced by a sword or a spear. As I approached the body, my arm came into view of the scene in front of me as it reached over to the victims' shoulders. I rolled him over onto his back and was overcome by a sense of familiarity. As his face revealed itself over its horizon, I realized this was my face. This was not any ordinary soldier, this soldier was me.

    In another dream I found myself in a place that could only be described as a long dark passageway. Countless doors could be found to the left and to the right of this infinite length of space that forever led to somewhere unknown. The doors would continually open, revealing their outline and flooding the corridor with an onslaught of light that expanded with the widening of the door and quickly disappearing as the door closed behind. I assumed that someone, unrevealed to me was entering or exiting. I could hear indiscernible conversations

taking place throughout the length of the long hallway. I confronted three individuals whose presence I felt but whose faces were hidden. They said I had to go back one more time through the door that I had just come from. These same dreams would be my frequent companion for years.

In exile, my father would say to me, "it is the responsibility of the son to be better than the father." These words bounced around my head as I was growing up. I often wondered if he was ever completely aware of the enormous responsibility he had placed on my shoulders with those words. Yet it drove me to build high personal expectations, to aim high and achieve career and personal success as quickly as possible. Father was a man that showed little emotion, but he is my best friend. He never actually said to me that he loved me, but these words seemed unnecessary and even redundant. There was a powerful understanding of love that was indisputable, even if it were not verbalized. I held him always as an example to follow, a man of logic, dignity, planning and intelligence that could solve all problems no matter how complex. As a young man, however, I knew that I had not met his expectations. I was a happy-go-lucky kid more comfortable contemplating my surroundings than achieving any higher goals. But what he didn't know was the hidden fact that I was up to his challenge; I just didn't know

how to achieve it. It was difficult for me to comprehend that it was somehow my responsibility to achieve some additional glory for the family and I had a very tough act to follow. To be fair though, I never gave any indication that his challenge concerned me in the least. I figured I just didn't understand the meaning, and I assumed that someday it would all reveal itself. In the meantime, Alejandro was a simply an inquisitive kid, who just couldn't grasp how he could possibly be better than his father.

      As a child, what was clear to me was that in order to understand my purpose in life and give it meaning, I would have to quickly leave the family in order to find my path to personal and family glory. After all, my maternal grandfather was making world headlines and everyone else had a role to play. After many hours of pondering the issue, I decided the best course of action would be to enlist in the United States Navy when I was seven years of age. My favorite uncle helped me fill out the enlistment application. He obviously never thought I would actually mail it, but to everyone's surprise, that is exactly what I did. Soon after, I received orders to report to a nearby naval training center to begin my chosen career. It was 1964 and the Vietnam War was in a state of constant escalation. The nation needed all the help it could muster, and at seven years of age, I was willing to answer that

call. I'll never forget the long telephone conversations between my father and the Navy department as he attempted to convince the American military authorities that I was not attempting to skip out on my responsibilities to my national duty, but that I was only a child! A bit embarrassed perhaps, they promptly dropped the issue. My goal of navigating the open seas would have to wait a little longer. The subsequent smile on my father's face told me that he had gotten a small glimpse of the kind of man that was buried inside me yearning to break free. In my own way I was letting him know that I had in fact heard his challenge of making something special of my life.

In the meantime, however, my afternoons were better spent in a constant state of world exploration; fascinated by everything around me. I was a crew cut, barefoot southern boy growing up in South Florida, sneaking out of my house to go fishing and explore lakes and rivers that would lead to the everglades. Everything was new and yet familiar to me at the same time. I'd follow a butterfly to see what was so attractive about a flower. I would follow the contours of the veins on a leaf and watched intently as the sunlight flickered through the branches of the trees near our home in Hialeah, Florida. I was not interested in academic lessons because those lessons were usually limited to coloring within some preconceived lines. I

had little patience for being quizzed or tested, but I did have an insatiable desire to learn. My lesson plans were just not in school, but outdoors in the world around me.

As I became older, I realized that in the aftermath of the Cuban revolution my contemplative nature had given me the time and focus to find the security I needed. I found comfort in solitude. I was never a loner in the true sense of the word, enjoying the company of many friends, but I did love my solitude and contemplative nature. It was important for me to know a little about everything, learning even at a young age that all things were complicated and connected to each other; the sunlight through the leaves, the flowers, the butterfly, the ground beneath me. I learned quickly by observing that colors were a simple reflection of light on objects. I came to understand that reality was a relative notion at best, and that the true colors of things were not exactly what our eyes could perceive. What we see with our own eyes is not entirely real. The color of a red rose is driven by the *rejection* of that spectrum of light that the eye then picks up and sees as red. It stood to reason then that the red rose was not red at all, but consisted of every color *except* red. And I began to ask myself what the world really looked like if I could "see" its true colors. A star that is sixty light years away may have collapsed and died, yet the night sky would present to me that beautiful star for the next sixty years since it would take that length of time for the last light emitted by the doomed star to reach us, revealing its demise. How could I then believe in the stars in heaven? This notion led me to trust my own feelings and not simply what my eyes necessarily revealed.

I was growing up in a new age, the so called Age of Aquarius, the middle of the twentieth century. Most of the family gathered and regrouped in Miami, Florida after the Cuban Diaspora with the exception of my maternal Grandfather Rafael. The decision to leave the island for the United States had given the family a new chapter in our long story and a shift towards the assimilation into an Anglo-society, forming a historical transition from generations of old and adding to the fabric of our family existence.

As I contemplated the world around me in the relative safety of exile, the Cold War was growing hotter and my mother's father, my grandfather Rafael, began to set the stage for what would become a counter-revolution. Grandfather Rafael Martinez would move to Central America shortly after landing in Miami as a refugee. The region of Central America would become a focal point for the Cold War struggle of the twentieth century. As a millionaire in Cuba, Grandfather Rafael had supported Castro's band of rebels with convoys of provisions to his mountain hideout and had been rewarded with the nationalization of his businesses empire once Fidel was in office. Rafael had moved to Guatemala not only to resurrect his own life, but also to plot his revenge against a Castro regime he had helped bring to power. We didn't know it then, but in the mind of Grandfather Rafael, his presence in Guatemala was a vital first step in his plans for war.

Chapter Two

The Cold War Comes Home

> "Let every nation know, whether it wishes us well or ill, that we shall pay any price, bear any burden, meet any hardship, support any friend, oppose any foe, in order to assure the survival and the success of liberty."
>
> JFK

The 1960's formed the peak of the Cold War between the United States and the Communist world. America and its allies were determined to contain the spread of communism and keep the Soviet empire confined to their borders and spheres of influence. It was a battle that had been growing in intensity when the family left the island. Throughout the world there was a fateful sense of inevitability. Several attempts to break out of this area of containment were tested by the Communist world with low-level conflicts, such as the siege of Berlin, the Korean War and the brewing Vietnam conflict. Both superpowers were oscillating their respective spheres of influence with the aim of controlling the very destiny of the world. Wherever the Communist bloc tested the West, the West would respond.

The rivalry between the Western and Eastern superpowers had been growing since the end of World War II, when the Soviet Union took possession of all the Eastern European territory it had liberated from Nazi Germany. Cuba was quickly becoming the latest pawn in this global geopolitical cat and mouse game, with the Soviet Union rejoicing at the opportunity to have such a valuable presence in America's backyard. Our island home, a mere ninety miles from Key West, thus became an outpost of the Communist movement, a beachhead and observation post right next to the heart of America.

In many ways this growing cold war was a conflict fed by misperceptions and fears.[3] From the American perspective, the world Communist movement was an empire whose desires were nothing short of world domination in the name of their Communist ideology, the very destruction of our way of life. While this was clearly an objective for many in Moscow, others from the Soviet Union viewed their possession of Eastern Europe as a protective measure to defend the motherland from the Western democracies, an ideology whose desires were nothing short of world domination in the name of democracy, the very destruction of

---

[3] Review: Perception and Paradox in the Cold War. Vol 21, No 3 (sept., 1993, Published by: John Hopkins University Press

their way of life. Moscow had pointed out that keeping Eastern Europe behind an "iron curtain," as Winston Churchill had proclaimed, created a buffer between the West and the Soviet heartland. They had seen Napoleon and then Hitler march into Russia through the same historical invasion route that moved through Poland and the other Eastern European nations towards Moscow. They used the fear of history to justify and legitimize their control and totalitarian regime. The control of the Eastern block of European nations was sold to anyone who would listen as a necessary possession to protect against any future attempt to invade their territory.

By 1960 the world was in crisis, on the brink of destruction. The period of time that coincided with our defection to the United States was marked by a high level of global fear. Francis Gary Powers American U-2 spy plane had been shot down by a Russian missile over the Soviet Union and was being tried in a Soviet courtroom on public display. It was also the year Soviet Premier Nikita Khrushchev was threatening the world by blockading Berlin, attempting to starve the West out of that city and solidifying their Iron Curtain position over Europe. Khrushchev had publicly cried out at the podium of the United Nations that the Soviet Union would "bury" America, as people in the United States were digging up their back-yards to build bomb shelters for the coming war, and children practiced ducking under their desks at the first sign of a nuclear explosion. Everyone was aware of the location of the nearest bomb shelter, and sirens went off periodically to test the warning systems that would announce pending doom. It was indeed a Cold War with only a simple miscalculation tipping the scale to a world of total annihilation.

Humanity was rapidly losing its innocence. We had, in fact, "become death, the destroyer of worlds"[4], as the words of the ancient Sanskrit text echoed in our collective consciousness. As a student of man, I saw this period in our history as the reign of political and ideological fanaticism. What I considered to be the first horseman of the apocalypse was galloping throughout the globe, followed closely by the second horseman, religious fanaticism, which would not be far behind in our history.

By the time of the Cuban revolution, the focus of the Cold War shifted from Europe to my island in a massive way. Three years after the revolution, several hundred thousand Cubans out of a population of six million left the country, along with most of the professional knowledge base of the island. Most of these were bankers, lawyers, physicians, businessmen and entrepreneurs, university professors, and

---

[4] J. Robert Oppenheimer

tens of thousands of others who left by any means available. The majority were from the upper and middle classes who saw themselves as financially worse off as a result of Castro's policies, their personal safety threatened by those who held their success a sin. Those who stayed on the island became increasingly dismayed when Castro reneged on his promise to hold free elections and reinstate the Constitution of 1940. The soaring expectations for Fidel Castro quickly collided with the harsh political reality that was Cuba. Castro reasoned that the national unity created by the revolution would be destroyed by the competing political parties engaged in an election, so he simply dismissed them as tools of social destruction.

To be sure, Cuban political history had been fraught with corruption and manipulation of power since the end of the War of Independence from Spain and repeated American intervention. But rather than seek to improve the system by finally implementing the Constitution of 1940 and establishing clear checks and balances to mitigate corruption, the specter of the past was used as a convenient excuse by Fidel Castro to consolidate and legitimize his own brand of dictatorial power.

My paternal Grandfather, Carlos Eduardo De La Cruz y Valdez-Montiel, a former Justice Minister, had stayed behind in Havana after we defected but was spared the wrath

of the revolutionary government. Even though he had been identified as a politician of a former regime, he was an elderly statesman, and considered no threat. His wife, my Grandmother Bárbara, would pass away in Cuba while we were in exile, and it would be several more years before we would be able to secure Grandfather Carlos's release from what amounted to house arrest on what remained of the De La Cruz compound.

While the family consolidated itself in exile, in Havana it was apparent that politicians who publicly disagreed with Castro's policy faced continual arrests. Ministers who questioned the wisdom of his policies were sacked and replaced by people who had proven their loyalty to him. These people were often young, inexperienced politicians who had fought with him in the Sierra Maestra Mountains. The Cuban revolutionary machine was beginning to consolidate its control over the population as we observed the energy in the delivery of Fidel Castro's fiery speeches to the multitudes.

My father had known Castro very well over the years, having attended University with him. Even as a child I had heard so much about the Fidel Castro that it seemed important to me to understand the man. I remember asking my father about his background and still recall his explanation. Father was convinced that the attribute of Castro's personal

background was a motivating factor in Castro's almost irrational behavior after attaining power. Indeed, understanding his background helped many Cubans deal with the aftermath of the disastrous revolution that everyone held with such high hopes when it began.

Fidel Castro's father was an illiterate Spaniard from Galicia named Ángel Castro. He arrived penniless to Cuba shortly before the turn of the century and left an estate that was worth more than half a million dollars when he died in 1956 at the age of eighty-six. The source of Ángel's fortune was built honestly by working on the properties of the United Fruit Company from 1904 to 1918. Cubans who knew Ángel, however, also knew him as a scoundrel who had no qualms about cheating anyone if he thought he could get away with it. His son, Fidel Castro, was an illegitimate child born in his father's house in Birán, in the Eastern Province of Oriente, born the same year as my father Eduardo in 1926.

The fact that Castro was illegitimate was not significant to most Cubans. Cubans attach little stigma to common law marriages, but they do, however, condemn bigamy, and Fidel was the product of a bigamous union between Ángel and a servant in his household. Fidel's father Ángel married a former mulatta schoolteacher by the name of María Argeta, around 1907 and had two children, Pedro and

Lidia. As he prospered, the Castro's brought into their home a Cuban servant girl named Lina Ruz Gonzales.

Lina Ruz bore Ángel seven children; Ángela, Ramón, Fidel, Raúl, Juana, Emma, and Agustina, all while he was still married to his first wife María. After all the children were born, at the urging of a neighbor and close friend, one Ricardo del Pino, Ángel Castro divorced María and married Lina. Many who have studied the behavior and motivation of Fidel Castro frequently point to this badge of family "dishonor" in his past as an explanation for his need to control, if not punish those he perceived to have socially looked down at him. With time, this justification for Castro's quest for power and behavior was adopted in the minds of most Cubans, surely those in exile. What is clear, however, is that the previously cosmopolitan city of Santiago de Cuba, whose social circles had treated Castro with much distain, has been systematically delegated to a second class status among Cuban cities in the last few decades by the Castro regime. How much truth there is to this notion of his past only Fidel Castro knows for sure.

As for the De La Cruz and Martinez family, arriving in the United States as refugees that October evening was like crossing over into another world. We had left a life of privilege, power and wealth to another land with no income

and no home. We arrived at Miami International Airport late in the evening of the 20th of October not knowing clearly where we would spend our first night in exile. Several aunts and cousins had departed Cuba on an earlier flight and had waited hours past our original time of arrival with the hope that we would emerge from the airport gate. When we did emerge, we were met by my mother's cousin Elisa, the daughter of my Aunt Mirta Martínez, one of my Grandmother Georgina's sisters.

  Family members were leaving the island from various exit points, all with instructions to rendezvous in Miami. Some left Cuba through the island of Jamaica, where they were held by the authorities until the proper bribes were paid to continue with their journey. Others went through the nation of Haiti. My grandmother's sister Alda and her husband Rubio organized an exodus of a group of family members including Aunt Irma and her husband and daughter Maggie, along with Great-Grandmother Amancia Verdecié Martínez, out of Cuba through Mexico. Shortly after my father's defection, my Uncle Rubio met briefly with Luis Buch, Fidel Castro's Chief of Staff and friend of the family. Buch introduced him to a very good document forger who could forge Mexican visas to leave the island. Eventually Rubio and his group of family members met up in Florida

with the rest of the Martínez clan, my mother's side of the family. As the days in exile progressed, family members united to provide assistance wherever it was possible. We made inquiries on employment and shelter; in short, we did what we could to survive. My father, mother, sister and I initially lived at the home of relatives until we found our own place in North Hollywood, Florida.

It had become apparent to my parents as the weeks and months went by that our stay in the United States was not going to be as short-lived as my mother had originally thought. The idea that a communist government would be allowed to survive ninety miles from the United States during the Cold War had been inconceivable, yet it appeared that that is exactly what was being allowed. The expected landing of U.S. Marines seemed to fade with each passing day.

To complicate matters, within six months of arriving into exile in Florida, my mother became pregnant. The couple who had at one time lost patience with their inability to begin a family after four years of marriage in Cuba suddenly was confronted with a new child during this moment of crisis in our lives. Unfortunately, they would lose this child to a miscarriage, and both Eduardo and Muñi would experience six other miscarriages over the next eight years, as children who were never meant to be known unsuccessfully attempted

to enter the world. No doubt the stress of exile had laid claim to more casualties than they thought.

  My father Eduardo, the former Cuban Ambassador, now found the only employment available to him was as a bag boy at an A&P supermarket store. What was most admirable to me about this fact was that he never hesitated in the least to take the job. The need to take care of his family far outweighed any perceived loss of prestige. It was clear that for him, dignity was not measured by what title you possessed, but by what actions you took and the decisions you made in the name of the many. In addition to the market, Eduardo also began to sell fencing, dinnerware and china, anything that would allow the family to move forward. My mother, who had spent tens of thousands of dollars each month at the most exclusive stores in Havana and New York, now worked for seventy-five cents an hour at a handbag factory gluing the handles of purses for American consumers. After working all day, she would come home with her hands encrusted with glue residue, completely exhausted from her day's labor.

  The A&P store proved to be more than just a source of needed cash for us. From the A&P my father would bring home food items that were not in the best of condition, sold to him at great discounts by the market. Steaks whose freezer burns had slightly discolored the meat, making them unsellable to the American consumer, became prized delicacies at our home. In addition, visits to the store during Christmas were particularly magical for both my sister and I. My father would walk us around the store during the Christmas holidays, showing us the various displays of toys set up above the frozen food section of the market. We would marvel at what we were seeing, pointing out our favorites, and to our surprise, Santa Claus somehow knew which ones we prized the most.

    The obvious struggle of my parents and the extended family seemed uneventful to us, the children. But even in struggle there was a collective sense of purpose, a feeling of hope, work and goals to be achieved. Eduardo would frequently tell me during this period in our life, with all the seriousness that he could muster, that while a government could take away your possessions and your positions in life, they could never remove your instincts and your education. Only you could defeat yourself by becoming complacent, lazy and apathetic. He warned me to learn and to study as much as I could, since these would someday become the only real tools of value to a man. Knowledge, combined with personal character, flavored with the love of family, were the only things a man really needed to succeed beyond all his

expectations. Anything short of that would lead to a hard and unnecessary struggle in life.

Grandfather Rafael and Grandmother Georgina Martínez also initially arrived in Miami, along with a box of my grandmother's personal jewels that were kept hidden from Castro's security at the Cuban airport. The jewels were probably worth several thousand dollars and would have been very helpful to our survival as a family. But in the confusion that was the Miami International Airport during the Cuban exodus, the box and all the jewels were lost or stolen at the airport terminal. Suffice to say that despite all the effort of Grandmother Georgina, her jewels had somehow become the latest victims of this turmoil. It was as if history were testing our abilities to rise from the ashes without the luxury of any tools or trinkets. It had somehow been decided that we were to regain our position in life without the ability to purchase our way, but to use only the sheer strength of our character to guide us.

Grandfather Rafael moved to the nation of Guatemala shortly after our arrival in Florida due to his lack of command of the English language as well as to tend to the last remnants of his business empire located in that Central American nation. The *Intercommunicadora Electrónica* the only remaining business of his former empire would provide a means to subsidize our immediate financial needs in Miami, while also supporting Rafael Martínez Púpo and Grandmother Georgina Martínez in Central America. But finances weren't the only motivation in my Grandfather's mind. This was initially an unaccompanied tour for Rafael. He could not afford to have his wife Georgina with him while he made the business flourish. In addition, he had other pressing plans that required his personal attention, and it would be best if the family were not around him. As a whole, the entire family was positioning itself in a great chess game of survival. We were all finding new means to live, new homes and in some instances, reinventing our very selves.

    The response of the general American population to this Cuban influx was met with some confusion. It was difficult for American society to open their doors to such a large group of new immigrants. There were cultural and language differences, differences that bred misunderstandings and fears. As a general rule, the Cubans that arrived in the early 1960's were educated and ambitious. There was a desire to create and build, to contribute to American society, matched only by the distaste by the initial wave of Cuban refugees at least, for social handouts such as welfare and food stamps. We refused to be a social burden to the American taxpayer, but just by being different we were nonetheless a threat.

    My father recalled the day a group of Seminole Indians walked into the A&P store dressed in native ceremonial garments for what I'm sure was some sort of tourist event. Eduardo by this time had been promoted to head cashier and was tending to a couple of elderly American retirees at the checkout stand when one of the ladies cried out to her friend, "Look, those must be those Cubans that are now arriving in large numbers". My father, diligently working the keys to the checkout machine, found himself stopping to respond; "No madam", he said, "those are Native Americans; I am one of the Cubans you are referring to".

Chapter Three

The Struggle to Regain Cuba

In the long history of the world, only a few generations have been granted the role of defending freedom in its hour of maximum danger. I do not shrink from this responsibility - I welcome it.

JFK

In an undisclosed wood-paneled conference room, a gathering of intense-looking bureaucrats held a meeting in a room adorned with pictures of American political luminaries displayed liberally on the walls. The room was in Langley, Virginia, the headquarters of the Central Intelligence Agency.

While the De La Cruz and Martinez family settled in Miami, in Washington, the CIA had come under orders from President Dwight Eisenhower to draft a top-secret policy paper calling for covert action against the Castro regime. By the end of the Eisenhower presidency, the plan for the overthrow of Fidel Castro had been approved. My father's prediction to his friend Luis Buch in Cuba that the U.S. Marines would soon land on the island to overthrow the regime seemed for all practical purposes to be on course. Washington was now in the planning stages for such an invasion. It was a plan that would soon bring Grandfather Rafael Martínez directly into the CIA payroll.

Washington was pregnant with what would become the "Cuba Project"[5] as the plan began its development stage at CIA headquarters. This was the largest and least-known CIA operation of the 1960's involving clandestine warfare, sabotage and political and economic subversion. The goal of the Cuba Project was to aim for a revolt in Cuba to overthrow the Communist regime. At over one billion dollars, the entire Cuba Project ended up also being one of the most expensive failures of the agency.

The plan developed for Cuba was similar to the policy that had worked so well in the overthrow of Guatemalan President Arbenz in 1954. It involved the creation of a Cuban government in exile as an initial propaganda offensive, followed by the nurturing and cultivation of internal resistance within the island. Even while this plan was being devised, the agency also began to recruit and train an outside invasion force to land troops on the island. The President of the United States had authorized thirteen million dollars to pay for the preparation of the invasion of Cuba using members of the Cuban exile community with American military support.

---

[5] Ted Shackley and Richard A. Finney (1992). <u>Spymaster: my life in the CIA</u>. Dulles, Virginia: Potomac Books, Inc..

Several additional proposals came from various sectors of American intelligence agencies setting in motion schemes that would undermine Castro's popularity with the Cuban people.[6] Some of these plots were bizarre in nature. One plan included the spraying of a hallucinogenic drug in a television studio in which Castro was about to appear, hoping his speech would slur, or contaminating his shoes with thallium, which the CIA believed would cause the hair in his beard to fall out. Thankfully, the CIA rejected these silly ideas in favor of arranging the assassination of Fidel Castro by negotiating a contract killing with Mafia crime bosses Johnny Roselli and Sam Giancana.

Using the Italian Mafia for a successful assassination would provide a credible cover story for the Agency. The Mob had lost millions in casino and hotel properties to the Cuban revolution. A successful assassination by the mob would have been credible given those circumstances, providing a Washington the ability to deny any involvement in the operation. A veteran agent of CIA counter-espionage was instructed to offer the Mafia $150,000 to kill Castro. But while the CIA worked on this angle of the Cuban problem, the Agency also began training 750 men in bases in Guatemala,

---

[6] Jack Anderson (1971-01-18). "6 Attempts to Kill Castro Laid to CIA". The Washington Post

Panama, Florida, Louisiana and Fort Meade for a land invasion of Cuba, which would become known as the Bay of Pigs Invasion.

President Kennedy on inauguration day, 1961

John F Kennedy was elected President of the United States in November of 1960. With his successful election, a copy of the Cuban invasion plan was delivered to the new President who immediately expressed surprise at the scale and sophistication of the operation. The plan called for a landing near the port city of Trinidad, which the CIA believed to be a hotbed of opposition to the Castro regime. The agency predicted that within four days of the landing, the invasion force would be able to recruit enough local volunteers to double in size. Airborne troops would first parachute behind enemy lines and secure the roads leading to the town. The rebel invasion force would then join up with the local guerrillas in the nearby Escambray Mountains.

At a meeting on the 11th of March, 1961, President Kennedy rejected the CIA's proposed scheme. He told them that the plan was "too well thought out"[7] and would be seen as an American creation. The new President then asked the CIA to draft a new plan that would be less spectacular and with a more remote landing site than Trinidad. His fear was that the plan was too sophisticated for the world to believe that it was a homegrown operation of Cuban exiles in conjunction with the disaffected Cuban people.

The agent in charge of the invasion was Richard Bissell, a seasoned CIA veteran. It was Bissell who resubmitted the invasion plans with a changed landing site from Trinidad to *Bahia de Cochinos* (Bay of Pigs). The Bay of Pigs landing site was a staggering eighty miles from the Escambray Mountains, making the linkup with the local guerillas difficult at best. What's more, the journey to the mountains from the beach head traversed an impenetrable and alligator-infested swamp. If the invasion failed, it would be difficult for the remaining forces to flee to the mountains to conduct guerrilla warfare. Facing the exile invasion force

---

[7] de Quesada, Alejandro; Walsh, Stephen. 2009. The Bay of Pigs: Cuba 1961. Osprey Elite series

would be the full force of the Cuban army with the Caribbean Sea behind them. As Richard Bissell explained to President Kennedy, the guerrilla fallback option had been removed from the operation. This, in conjunction with the unsatisfactory location of the landing site, made the operation appear *sufficiently amateurish*[8] to provide Washington with plausible deniability over its involvement in the invasion plans.

What was most staggering about this change in plans was the fact that the original invasion plan had been approved by Dwight Eisenhower, the supreme Allied commander during World War II. It amazes me that the administration of John F Kennedy would so dramatically change such an important and well thought-out plan. But this was not by itself the reason for the failure of the Bay of Pigs invasion.

By early 1961 the anti-Castro underground was performing at peak efficiency. Some of our boys of the underground raced in cars through the streets distributing anti-Castro literature. Bombs began to explode in parts of the city, and fires broke out in various places at the same time. The American invasion plan, code named "Pluto," had set D-day for April 17, 1961. Even though it was poorly planned, it could still have worked had two other things not occurred that

---

[8] Bissell, Richard M. Jr., with Jonathan E. Lewis and Frances T. Pudlo. Reflections of a Cold Warrior: From Yalta to the Bay of Pigs

guaranteed its failure. The first, which is not widely talked about, was the extent of infiltration of Castro agents into the exile community in Miami, and in the halls of the U.S. government itself. When the plan were finalized in Washington D. C., a copy of the invasion orders were hand-carried by a CIA agent from Langley to the invasion force's base of operations just outside of Guatemala City where Grandfather Rafael Martínez Púpo had a residence. Two days before the invasion was to begin, the agent boarded a commercial flight to Central America and changed planes in Mexico City. In Mexico, the CIA operative carrying the plans disappeared. He surfaced the next day in Havana, the day before the invasion was to take place. Castro, who had been prepared for the invasion in the port city of Trinidad, now began to move troops to the Bay of Pigs.

To complicate matters, President Kennedy had stated in a press conference on April 12, without consulting any military adviser, that there would not, under any conditions be an intervention in Cuba by U.S. armed forces. His government, he said, would make sure that there are no Americans involved.

As the time for the Bay of Pigs invasion grew near, sabotage by the anti-Castro Cuban underground increased inside Cuba. The Hershey sugar mill warehouse and two confiscated Woolworth stores were set afire. On April 14, Cuba's largest department store and my mother's shopping passion, *El Encanto* department store, was burned to the ground by the rebels. Throughout the island, towns and cities resounded to explosions as government buildings and plants were bombed in anticipation of the American-backed offensive.

Bay of Pigs invasion force in formation at base camp Guatemala. Site later used by Grandfather Rafael Martínez Púpo for "Commando Mambise" training.

For sure, some members of the Cuban underground were CIA-organized groups, but the majority of the resistance was disaffected members of the Cuban population that had felt betrayed by Castro and his failure to deliver on his promises.

One of the most active groups of the Cuban underground were the members of the *Catholic Action Group*[9], a church organization of volunteers, whose primary desire was to help their fellow faithful become better Christians. This group now turned militant against the atheist Castro regime, joining with others in the underground to plot against him. As a means of identification, the activists in Cuba used a simple drawing of a fish, copied from the early Christians of Rome.

Had there been adequate coordination between the underground and the invasion force, things would have resulted better than they actually did. Castro had every reason to fear such freedom fighters. Day after day the Cuban cities had resounded to explosions as government buildings and plants were sabotaged. The guerilla activities had far surpassed those of the anti-Batista underground in 1958.

In Washington on the 13th of April, Kennedy asked Richard Bissell how many B-26 bombers were going to be used in the operation, to which Bissell replied, sixteen. The President dismissed that number and ordered that only eight bombers be used. Bissell knew that the invasion could not succeed without adequate air cover; nevertheless, the orders stood. The following day the bombers went into action against Cuba's airfields. Two days later, five merchant ships carrying

---

[9] Interview with Cuban Ambassador Eduardo C. delaCruz

1,400 Cuban exiles of what was called *Brigade 2506* landed on the beach at the Bay of Pigs.

The night of the invasion, eager-faced paratroopers stood waiting for the aircraft cabin light to turn green signaling they were over the desired drop zone. One by one the men jumped into the darkness below as the clouds swirled by the open hatch of the aircraft. The first stage of the invasion had been spectacularly successful. The three roads across the swamp had been commandeered by paratroopers, and they had taken control of the Girón airport, their primary objective. Several hundred members of Castro's militia and citizens of Girón joined the liberation forces, asking for weapons to join in the fight against the Castro dictatorship.

The invasion proceeded as scheduled under the assumption that Castro would not have sufficient time to establish a defensive position around the landing site and that the expected uprising of the Cuban population would more than offset this "setback" in security. On April 17 at 12:05a.m., the first assault troops landed on the shore.

The second and most important cause of the failure of the landing was that the promised American air cover from the carriers just off the coast of the Bay of Pigs were held back at the last minute by the Kennedy White House. Castro's air force, which was supposed to have been eliminated by

American pilots, survived the reduced number of American sorties designed to destroy them. Castro's air force had been cut in half, but he still had at least two jets and two B-26 bombers remaining. With the landing of the exile force, Castro's planes came screaming in, guns and rockets blazing. He used them with a relentless accuracy on a force that had no place to go from the established beachhead. The remaining Castro pilots quickly picked off the exile troops and destroyed all their supply ships at the landing site.

The beachhead was billowing with smoke. The Free Cuban Commanders on the beach repeatedly asked for air support. Radios were heard loudly and desperately behind American lines out at sea, "Where is the air cover?!?"[10] As these desperate calls for air cover came over the airwaves, several American pilots actually considered disobeying orders and striking out in defense of a landing force they knew they had helped create and were being left to fend for themselves in the moment of their most dire need. Admiral Burke, commander of the American fleet off site of the landing zone had repeatedly asked for permission to land a detachment of Marines and place American forces in action. He was repeatedly denied.

---

[10] Pfeiffer, Jack B. 1979. Official History of the Bay of Pigs Operation, Vol.I Air Operations, Part 1

Toward the end of the battle, an exasperated Admiral Burke issued a last request to allow a single U.S. destroyer to approach the shore and lay down a barrage of gunfire on Castro's forces. The President's response was that if they did what the Admiral was suggesting, then the U.S. would be involved in the conflict. The Admiral's response to his President was clear, *"We are involved, sir. God damn it, Mr. President, we can't let those boys be slaughtered there!"*[11] At one point, Washington did relent and sent out a squadron of fighter aircraft in order to avoid a total massacre. The appearance of American fighters in Cuban airspace immediately encouraged the troops at the landing site, and for a brief moment, the Castro air force disappeared, refusing to challenge the superior skills of the Americans. Unfortunately, rather than strafe the enemy or bomb the Castro tanks, the American aircraft dipped their wings back and forth in a salute to the free Cuban troops. They made a few circles around the invasion site and quickly withdrew back to the carriers. Shortly after this, the Cuban air force reappeared and the invasion force was finished.

The Cuban underground did the best they could, but there was little coordination with the Americans or the CIA.

---

[11] Bohning, Don (2005). The Castro Obsession: U.S. Covert Operations Against Cuba, 1959–1965. Washington, D.C.: Potomac Books, Inc

Fidel Castro with his tank forces at the Bay of Pigs landing site
http://www.youtube.com/watch?v=ROIXpuKkHpw&feature=related

Many small groups, trained and supplied with explosives by the CIA, managed to infiltrate into Cuba from Central America. Unbelievably, they never received the agreed upon signal from the United States to go into action.

In Havana, members of the underground were being systematically rounded up and slaughtered. Approximately a hundred thousand people had been rounded up and imprisoned throughout the island on the days following the invasion fiasco. The lists had been compiled by the secret street-corner "Vigilance Committees," the dreaded "Committee for the Defense of the Revolution".

In the aftermath of the invasions collapse several hundred members of the Cuban underground found refuge in the Italian embassy in Havana. When access to the Latin American embassies were under strict surveillance, the Italian embassy gates were opened again and again to admit men and boys who would have otherwise been shot had they been captured. Many Cubans owe a debt of gratitude to the Marquis Marchioness de Teodoli, the Italian Ambassador and his Hungarian wife who made it their personal mission to give asylum to members of the underground who were able to reach their embassy.[12] The experience was not a new one for the Marchioness, who had saved more than fifty lives in Budapest when the Soviets smashed that rebellion of 1956. Among those taking refuge at the Italian Embassy was a young boy who a few days earlier had helped set the fire which had totally destroyed the El Encanto department store.

The Cuban community in South Florida was aghast. How was it that Washington allowed this mission to fail? In fact, there were elements of the U.S. Government that were gambling that a failure would lead to victory. The director of the CIA, Allen Dulles, felt at the time of the change in plans to the Bay of Pigs that the invasion was doomed to failure, but he believed Kennedy would order a full-scale invasion once he realized this failure was upon them. According to the book, *The Very Best Men*, by Evan Thomas, some old CIA hands

---

[12] Interview with Cuban Ambassador Eduardo C. delaCruz

believe that (Richard) Bissell was setting a trap to force U.S. intervention. Within seventy-two hours of the landing at the Bay of Pigs, all the invading troops had been killed, wounded or had surrendered. President Kennedy took full responsibility for the failure of the invasion, but in the end, it was the CIA director that was forced to resign. Castro gave credit to his air force for having turned the tide and condemned militias units for having joined the invaders.

Clearly, the American's failure at the Bay of Pigs in the end had the opposite effect it intended. In August 1961 Richard Goodwin, speech writer for President Kennedy, had a chance meeting with Che Guevara during an Inter-American Economic and Social conference in Uruguay. During this brief meeting, Che sarcastically asked Goodwin to relay to President Kennedy his heartfelt thanks for the Bay of Pigs invasion.[13] It seems that Castro only had a loose grip on the Cuban nation, which was undergoing significant economic and internal rivalry. The Bay of Pigs invasion actually solidified Castro's hold on power as the hero who had rebuffed the most powerful nation in the world. The debacle of the Bay of Pigs had elevated Castro to the pinnacle of his power and prestige.

---

[13] The Brilliant Disaster: JFK, Castro, and America's Doomed Invasion of Cuba's By Jim Rasenberger page 350.

Captured Brigade 2506 Troops at the Bay of Pigs landing site.

That same year in Havana, my paternal Grandmother Barbara passed away. Grandfather Carlos Eduardo De La Cruz and my aunt Angelina huddled together, sheltered from a steady rain under a large black umbrella. It was a relatively small group, given the fact that most family members had gone into exile. It was a Tuesday, at nine in the morning on a day and month that will remain anonymous out of respect for my father Eduardo, who wished never to know the exact day his mother Bárbara Mesa De La Cruz was buried in the family crypt. She had died of an enlarged heart, wounded; I'm sure, by the burden of her own history. My grandfather Carlos was inconsolable given the fifty-eight years he had spent with his wife and the fact that many of her children could not be present to mark this occasion at his side.

For those there, the funeral site created a difficult image, yet while there was great sadness, there was also a sense… an almost indiscernible sound of joy in those present, an understanding that Bárbara had crossed over to a place where she would finally meet up with her parents Sixta and Mateo Mesa. She had not seen them since she became lost at six years of age when she became separated from them during the War for Independence from Spain more than fifty years before. It was another dark period in Cuban history that now belonged only to the past. She had become separated and lost during the roundup of humanity by General Weyler's Spanish troops as they gathered Cubans on their way to the concentration camps. In the aftermath of that war, she would never see her parents again.

Given the separation with her parents at such an early age, a sense of "apartness" from family was understood and familiar to Bárbara while she was alive, so the absence of so many of her children during her funeral would not have had the impact on her that it would on most. The separation between life and after-life could not have been more blurred on that rainy day in 1961. For as those present were witnessing a saddened old man with his daughter standing in the rain observing a casket being positioned in the crypt, an unseen reunion of utter joy could be felt alongside them as three ecstatic spirits of the Mesa family finally celebrated a reunion, bathed in the light of a long-anticipated and overdue embrace.

In Miami meanwhile, my mother had taken ill to the point that her continued employment at the handbag factory was in serious doubt. The financial impact of losing a second source of income meant the family could not keep up with our house payment. The result was the loss of our home. It was a setback for sure, and despite the attempts by the bank working feverishly to assist us in reorganizing our loans, the income stream was just not there to support that goal.

Thankfully, a co-worker of my father at the A&P supermarket mentioned to Eduardo that his father owned a small home which he thought we could rent for seventy-five dollars a month. The family financial situation was abysmal when we moved to what could only be described as a dilapidated shack. My mother would recall the extensive cleaning that was required to make the house livable, scrubbing on her hands and knees to remove the encrusted excrement that lay on the bathroom floors. Whenever the washing machine was on, the floor flooded from underneath the tiles. While this was clearly a problem, we made do with what we had. Things were indeed dire, and at one point the only thing available to eat in the house was a small can of Vienna sausages which both my sister and I consumed as our dinner. We would see several nights like that when my parents did not have a meal.

    Growing up in Miami, I had my own interests and concerns that were far different from those of my parents. From my perspective, this was a new neighborhood that needed extensive exploring, and I was just the man to do the job. As usual, my primary objective was to identify and understand the personalities of all the homes around us, while at the same time search for the most perfect flower to bring to my mother. As it happened, our neighbor had a flowering bush which produced the most exquisite flower I had ever seen. This prized plant was delicately tended by the neighbor's wife with great care. And as you would expect, the flower became my prized choice for my mother. I was just not aware that this bush only produced a single flower each year. I had never heard up to that point such anger and language in an adult voice when our neighbor discovered me a few moments after committing the crime. I remember running for my life, dashing behind the house into the laundry room for any protection I could find that would shelter me from the incoming rounds that were surely being fired by my neighbors.

  My actions that afternoon caused an international incident as my father found it necessary to restrain my mother when they both heard the neighbor yell, "These Cubans, if you move your eyes away for a moment they will steal your shirt". With time and diplomatic patience, my sister Liz and I made friends with the neighbor's daughter, who for some inexplicable reason ended up spending an unusual amount of time at our home. Eventually, the neighbor came around or had no choice but to accept us as the human beings we were and all was well again.

  The explorations of my world led me to the pleasure of climbing trees, making friends and identifying which house in the community was the scariest place on the planet. There was this one home with an overgrown front garden that made the place appear to be nestled in its own jungle. To complete the creepiness, a disheveled and scruffy old man lived there alone. Entering the grounds of this home quickly became the main test of courage during many a Halloween night.

  One particular day, after a healthy rain had fallen in the neighborhood, I was at the street corner tossing pebbles into a recently formed pond. This old neighbor came out of his house about a half a block away from my position. Turning in my direction, the creepy man yelled "hey kid!" That was enough for me to dump my remaining supply of pebbles and dash towards my home, passing my bewildered mother as I charged into the house, into my bedroom, and straight under my bed. I was there for about five minutes and only came out when I wondered what my Grandfather Rafael would say if he saw me hiding under the bed. No doubt he would have roared with that jolly laughter that I remember he always had.

Grandfather Rafael was becoming more involved with the CIA efforts to overthrow the Castro government. The failure of the Bay of Pigs invasion had humiliated the Kennedy brothers, and now more than ever, they wanted Castro removed from office whether by palace revolt, popular uprising or assassination. An interdepartmental group was formed by the administration headed by the President's brother Robert Kennedy, to supervise the work of the CIA towards the goal of deposing Castro. The group also included National Security Advisor McGeorge Bundy and CIA director Allan Dulles, along with members of the Joint Chiefs of Staff.

With the failure of the Bay of Pigs invasion, Bobby Kennedy settled on a strategy of economic sabotage as the key to the downfall of Castro. It was this new strategic campaign that brought Grandfather Rafael Martínez Púpo into the CIA fold. At a meeting in November, 1961, Kennedy accused

Bissell of not doing anything about getting rid of Castro and the Castro regime.[14] Ironically, it was President Kennedy and his brother Bobby that had significantly changed the invasion plans to a point that it guaranteed the failure to achieve the objective they now most coveted. After showing a level of timidity never before seen in American foreign policy, Bobby Kennedy now was calling for boom and bang all over the island. During that same November meeting, the task of overthrowing the Castro regime was given to the CIA station in Miami under the code name "Task Force W".

The CIA station in Miami was known cryptically as JMWAVE, and it would eventually become the CIA's largest station in the hemisphere. It quickly tapped into the angry community of Cuban exiles in Miami itching to regain their homeland. Operating from 1961 through 1968, JMWAVE, also known as the "Wave station" or the "Miami station,"[15] resided in building 25 on the South Campus of the University of Miami. The agency headquarters was located in a heavily wooded 1,571-acre tract of land holding containing numerous

---

[14] McGeorge Bundy, <u>Memorandum of Meeting with President Kennedy</u>, White House, Washington, February 8, 1961

[15] Ted Shackley and Richard A. Finney (1992). <u>Spymaster: my life in the CIA</u>. Dulles, Virginia: Potomac Books, Inc..

buildings that were labeled as belonging to a corporation called the "Zenith Technological Enterprises."

The station chief of the Miami operation was a man named Ted Shackley, who became personally committed to the cause of overthrowing Fidel Castro in an operation that became known as "Operation Mongoose." Shackley brought on board a group of CIA operatives that had previously been involved with the overthrow of President Jacobo Arbenz of Guatemala in 1954. This included David Atlee Phillips and E. Howard Hunt, later to be made famous as part of Nixon's Watergate burglar team. (On his deathbed in 2007, Howard Hunt would name David Atlee Phillips as a participant in the Kennedy assassination, but that is a totally different story).[16]

Very soon after organizing Operation Mongoose, paramilitary teams of the CIA were moving in and out of the island, often gathering intelligence from Cuban fishing trawlers. The new directive from the White House was clear; Bobby Kennedy wanted to fully implement the Miami station's full arsenal of paramilitary operations against major industrial targets throughout the island. Specifically, Kennedy was looking for unconventional warfare techniques, low-level harassments and the avoidance of any major action such as

---

[16] Hedegaard, Erik (April 5, 2007). "The Last Confessions of E. Howard Hunt". Rolling Stone. Archived from the original on June 18, 2008

strategic bomber sorties targeting Cuba's industrial base. Thus began a guerilla warfare campaign designed to take the war to the central government of Cuba by small but painful attacks countrywide, causing Cuban government forces to disperse throughout the island in response to multiple incidents of sabotage and destruction. The intent of the strategy was to give the Cuban people a sense that organized resistance was widespread throughout the Island, motivating more of the population to join in their own form of rebellion.

In some cases the plan worked, but it was frequently slow to react. Washington's "special group" under Bobby Kennedy created a system of such tight operational control that even a small attack required a fifty page operational plan. The system built itself several levels of second guessing that made the operation's flow cumbersome at best. But several successful operations were nevertheless carried out inside the island.

By the spring of 1962, JMWAVE employed more than two hundred CIA officers managing over three thousand Cuban agents. At their disposal was a navy of over one hundred craft, including the 174-foot "Rex," carrying onboard the latest electronic equipment and 40-millimeter and 20-millimeter cannons. The CIA station also had a large number of V-20 Swift craft and access to F-105 Phantoms from nearby Homestead Air Force Base.

The family in Miami was not fully aware of what Grandfather Rafael was doing with the CIA, certainly not me. I was more concerned with my immediate issues and my new school. My first day of class at the Immaculate Conception School, a private Catholic School, was unbelievably stressful. I wrapped myself around my father's pant leg in a pointless effort to avoid the grasp of the nun who so much wanted to take me away. Eventually I surrendered to this robed higher authority, and once inside, I explored my surroundings and the multitudes of other children while the nun and my father spoke outside. It seemed silly to just stand there in front of the class, so I took the first desk on the second row to sit down. A girl suddenly started to laugh, saying out loud, "look, he's sitting in the girls' row" to which other children also began to laugh. Clearly, I thought, this was setting up to be a very long and difficult academic experience.

At the Catholic School I found that I was careless, and my mind would often wonder into daydreams that would tend to land me in trouble for one thing or another in school. Most of the time my troubles were caused by my uncanny ability to continuously spill my milk from my desk during snack periods. It seems the wooden desk that held a slight slant and opened to reveal a storage place for our books had little traction to hold a thermos of the milky coffee I would bring to class. It was not unusual in Cuba to have what we called "café con leche". I would have it cold most of the time at school. Decades later Americans would discover this drink and give it a French sounding *café late* name, but for me in 1962, spilling it was the reason I frequently spent endless periods of time facing the corner wall in punishment as the class continued behind me.

Sometimes I would be held behind after class to stare at this corner wall after the final bell would ring, and I would cry at the notion that the bus would leave without me, rendering me a homeless orphan forever. Like clockwork, my sister Liz had quickly learned the routine and pattern of my absence from the bus. If I was not at the bus stop, that meant I was standing duty at the classroom corner wall and she would set out on a mission to negotiate my release. Since I was not allowed to turn my head away from the wall, I could only monitor her progress in the negotiations with the unmerciful nuns through the sound of her voice.

It was also in the third grade of this school that I fell in love for the very first time in my life. Her name was Sister Emanuel, an angelic looking nun, an exquisitely beautiful woman whose full length white robes would flow and trail a split second behind her whenever she turned around to face the class. I was young and completely unaware that we could not view nuns this way.

  The school had a great impact on my life. I was focusing on establishing my own belief system, recognizing that our personal beliefs formed the texture of our future lives. As I observed, I learned that such a process is inherently an internal one, with each belief beginning as a choice. On a global scale, diverse belief systems can cause cultures to draw boundaries, and ideologies to clash. On a personal level, what I was learning to believe about myself would appear later in my life *as* my life. But as I was learning to discover myself, I had the best of times doing so, even while the world was in the height of the Cold War and experiencing the worst of times.

  The school provided me with structure and organization. We wore uniforms and maintained common rituals and church events. My class, like all others, would march with our hands clasped together as if in prayer, making our way to the school cafeteria like some tribal calling; hot dogs with mustard only on Tuesdays, and sloppy joes on Thursdays. I had a friend whose claim to fame was an ability to fold his eyelids backwards, holding them that way until he folded them back. I experienced first Holy Communion and my first confession and I still remember the smell of the carpet and the deafening sound of the silence I heard in that little confession room while I waited for the small door to slide open so I could reveal my "sins" to a total stranger. Confession, to me, was kind of like homework. I had to quickly come up with things to say to the priest and it was difficult at such a young age to search for anything really good. And in the end, it really didn't seem to matter anyway because while having no sins was unacceptable, and too many sins were problematic, any sin rendered the same sentence of *Hail Mary's* and *Our Father*'s as the price for my freedom. I had no idea of the war drums being played in Washington, or Havana, or what a Soviet Union was all about. My world had its borders, and while I wasn't completely oblivious to what lay beyond, my focus was in laying the foundation for my own existence.

What I concluded from those early years as I grew older, was that life itself moves continually as an energy that flows through us, circulating to the rest of the world, and then returning back to us once more. The world operates through the universal law of cause and effect. Your health, your spiritual community, your family require an energy flow of give and take. If you stop giving in one area, be it the quest for knowledge, enthusiasm, food and rest, the quest for inner peace, love and nurturing, that part of your life suffers, giving you back little in return. Like a stream, energy must keep circulating to stay alive and vital; otherwise it begins to grow stagnant. Giving and receiving forms a circle and a circle has no end. For each area of our lives to thrive and grow, we need to give freely and receive with gratitude.

It also became clear from my experiences that wealth and power are illusions that can vanish and reappear, and it's the spirit inside you that truly lasts forever. Those who had not learned this could never really move forward; they were condemned to run in place in life, thinking they are running through their life experiences but never really making any headway. It's an exhausting waste of time and opportunities. Some of those people lived around us all the time. My sister was told by her best girlfriend, for example, that her mother had forbidden her from playing with her because she could no longer associate with "Cubans". That level of ignorant discrimination was difficult for some, especially those that experienced it. For some reason, I was either immune to it or too young to understand it, but with time, Cubans began to contribute and expand the economic base of South Florida. Eventually, the largest banks and construction companies, countless small businesses and restaurants and night clubs were owned and operated by Cubans, providing tens of thousands of Americans with new jobs.

As I learned about these human issues, the war against Castro was continuing to move forward in a sort of parallel existence. Several dozen commando groups involving elements of the large Cuban refugee community emerged out of project Mongoose as part of this war against Castro. The most notable of these in those early years was a group called Alpha 66, who launched several raids on Cuba. These included attacks on port installations and foreign shipping. The Russian merchant ship "Baku" was sunk, and their activities were reported in *Life Magazine*. Some members of the Alpha 66 members had been active in the Student Revolutionary Directorate, the same organization that had been formed by former Cuban President Grau San Martín in protest against the rule of Fulgencio Batista. The Student Directorate had risen in opposition to Castro's Communist views and many of its leaders had fled to the United States. Many of these anti-Castro groups were very active inside and out of Cuba.

http://www.youtube.com/watch?v=VMtsbPQSGLw

An equal number of exile groups, however, had been compromised with double agents and informants for the Castro regime. The Cold War cat and mouse game had come to roost on the shores of Miami and in the narrow waterways that separated the United States from Cuba. Bobby Kennedy was still demanding action in Cuba, but Castro always seemed to be one step ahead. Something always seemed to go wrong with these sabotage operations. All this changed with the recruitment of Grandfather Rafael Martínez Púpo by Ted Shackley's Miami CIA station.

Chapter Four

The Missile Crisis

"It was a perfectly beautiful night், as fall nights are in Washington. I walked out of the president's Oval Office, and as I walked out, I thought I might never live to see another Saturday night."

— Secretary of Defense Robert S. McNamara

The Central Intelligence Agency had decided that a new operational cell distinct from any Miami group currently involved in Operation Mongoose needed to be created. It was essential that this new group be a compartmentalized cell as far away from Castro's influence as possible.

A former naval officer by the name of Bob Simons, who was tasked by the CIA to recruit underwater demolition teams, was placed in charge of the operation. Dave Morales, an American Army officer of Mexican descent who had been a CIA operative for years and had been a key player in the overthrow of the Guatemalan government of Arbenz, was placed in charge of recruiting the leadership of the team.

In his book *Spymaster; My Life in the CIA,* Theodore Shackley wrote of the recruitment of Grandfather Rafael

Martínez Púpo for this operation at a meeting in the Hotel Roosevelt in New Orleans:

> "Dave Morales produced a candidate whom he had known in Havana-Rafael M(artinez), a man who had become a multimillionaire in business in Cuba, who had seen all his properties confiscated by Castro, and who was now traveling extensively throughout Central America as a representative of various American companies. We ran our usual checks on M(artinez), and Dave and I then sat down to talk with him. He was just what the doctor ordered: a discreet, dedicated, patriotic Cuban who wanted to do something against Castro, but who, because of his prolonged absences from Miami, had not been drawn into professional revolutionary circles…We recruited him, and he, Dave, and I then put our heads together to try to find a name for the group. We were all in agreement that "commandos" had to be part of it, but "Commandos *what*"? Finally, M(artinez) remembered that the Cuban resistance fighters against Spain had called themselves "Mambises." There was no need to look any further. The "Commandos Mambises" were born."

One of the prominent members of the Mambise organization was the former Army Chief of Staff for Batista, General Manuel Pedraza. General Pedraza had attempted to assassinate the dictator Batista. After his attempt to kill Batista failed, the General would ironically rejoin forces with Batista in a futile attempt to destroy Castro's revolution. Shortly before Castro took power, the General's son had been stopped and murdered by Castro's rebels when his identity became known. Now in exile in 1962, he and my Grandfather Rafael

Grandfather Rafael Martínez Púpo, third from right. General Manuel Pedraza, former Army Chief of Staff of Fulgencio Batista is second from right at a CIA meeting in New Orleans.

Martínez Púpo joined forces under the CIA umbrella that was the Mambise Commandos to plot Castro's overthrow.

The main leader of the Mambise Commando[17] group was a former Cuban Air Force officer named Major Manuel Villafana, code named "Ignacio", a Cuban General Patton known for his spit-and-polish sternness, who had commanded the Bay of Pigs air force. The Mambise Commandos were considered by the CIA director of Naval Operation, Gordon

---

[17] A Guide to the Rafael Martínez Pupo Papers Relating to Comandos Mambises. Finding aid created by Margarita Vargas-Betancourt. University of Florida Smathers Libraries - Special and Area Studies Collections. November 2011

Campbell to be the elite, the Green Berets of the Secret War against the Castro regime.

Manuel Villafana

Mambise Commando leader "Ignacio," Cuban Major Manuel Villafana

At the insistence of Major Villafana, all members of the commando teams were paid only three hundred dollars a month by the CIA, a pittance of a figure even for the time. This was done in order to motivate the members to be driven by hate rather than money. The training for the Mambise Commandos had been an intensive effort in both the Florida Everglades and a camp just outside of New Orleans and Guatemala. By late 1962, Commando operations inside Castro's Cuba had begun.

A group of men dressed in black, their faces blackened by camouflage waited almost impatiently onboard the "Rex", a converted World War II ship. It was just before midnight, and the relatively calm waves barely rippled as they washed ashore. Far off to the east, a lighthouse flashed long and short, marking the entrance to a bay. The large ship used its crane on the aft deck to lower the speedboat as the men clamored down the netting to board the crafts.

The Rex was JMWAVE's flag ship. It was a converted sub chaser flying the Nicaraguan flag and commanded by Captain Alejandro Brooks. The crews were experienced Cuban sailors of the former Batista regime on the CIA's payroll. The Rex's 40-mm naval cannon and 57-mm recoilless rifle were clearly visible as darker shadows against the night sky. Quickly and quietly, the Commandos got underway for a mission against the Castro regime.

The Headquarters for the Commandos was decentralized. Castro's men were all over the Miami exile community vigilantly watching for any organized exile activity, it became important for the Mambises not to be based anywhere in particular. When a mission was scheduled, each commando would receive a phone call that was followed by the arrival of a nondescript CIA van to pick them up. They would quietly proceed to the West Palm Beach pier where the Rex was tied up as an asset of the "Sea Key Shipping Company," a CIA front company whose address was a Miami post office box number.

In the Soviet Union, the Kremlin was actively debating how to best protect this new Cuban asset against Washington incursions. Given the Bay of Pigs invasion and the escalating CIA plans to overthrow the Cuban revolutionary regime, Soviet Premier Nikita Khrushchev sent Castro as much assistance as he was able. By October, 1962, the Soviet empire had 40,000 soldiers, 1,300 field pieces, 700 anti-aircraft guns, 350 tanks and 150 jets in Cuba in order to deter another invasion.

In September of 1962, American U-2 spy planes discovered the construction of Soviet surface-to-air missiles in Cuba. In addition to these missile sites, there was a significant increase in Soviet shipping traffic arriving at various Cuban ports, which the CIA in Langley became convinced were carrying supplies of weapons. With surface-to-air missiles classified as offensive weapons, President Kennedy immediately issued a complaint to the Soviet Union informing Khrushchev that the United States would not tolerate such weapons in Cuba capable of shooting down U-2 spy planes. It was also evident that Kennedy had other concerns. The recent loss of the Bay of Pigs invasion had placed the President in a difficult political position. Elections were to take place for the United States Congress in two month's time and public opinion had fallen to its lowest point since JFK had become

President. Kennedy feared that any trouble over Cuba would remind voters of the Bay of Pigs disaster, causing the Democratic Party to lose even more votes.

Pollsters showed that over 62 per cent of the population was unhappy with Kennedy's policies on Cuba, and as a result, the Republicans made every effort to make Cuba the main issue in the Presidential campaign. This was probably in Kennedy's mind when he decided to restrict the flights of the U-2 planes over the island. Pilots were also told to avoid flying the whole length of the Cuban nation, as a cautious Kennedy hoped this would ensure that a U-2 plane would not be shot down.

With the Bay of Pigs fiasco and the Kennedy administration's perceived or actual indecisiveness, the Soviet empire believed that it could place offensive nuclear missiles in Cuba and effectively alter the strategic balance of power. The Cuban Missile Crisis was about to begin, and it would be the closest the world would ever come to nuclear war.

Motivating the Soviet Union to place offensive nuclear missiles in Cuba was the fact that in 1962, the Soviet Union was well behind the United States in the arms race. Soviet nuclear missiles could only reach Western Europe; while the United States had intercontinental ballistic missiles (ICBM's) capable of targeting Soviet territory from the United States as well as an assortment of medium-range nuclear weapons in nearby Turkey. Placing intermediate-range missiles in Cuba would give the Soviet Union the ability to accurately target American assets and population centers while doubling the Soviet strategic arsenal and providing a real deterrent to a potential U.S. attack against the Soviet Union. Also, the experience of the Bay of Pigs invasion in 1961 had convinced Castro that a second invasion against his regime was inevitable.

In late September of 1962, a CIA agent in Cuba overheard Castro's personal pilot tell another man in a bar that Cuba now had nuclear weapons.[18] U-2 spy-plane photographs also showed that unusual activity was taking place at San Cristóbal. Reconnaissance photographs soon revealed Soviet missiles under construction in that region. However, it was not until October 15th that photographs were taken that revealed that the Soviet Union was placing long range missiles in island.

Kennedy called an emergency meeting of the Executive Committee of the National Security Council to discuss this growing threat to the security of the United States. Fourteen men attended the meeting and included military

---

[18] Mindsets and Missiles: A Firsthand Account of the Cuban Missile Crisis (page 49). By Kenneth Michael Absher

leaders, experts on Latin America, representatives of the CIA, cabinet ministers and personal friends whose advice Kennedy valued. Deliberations were intense at the White House situation room. At the height of the crisis, the National Security Council considered several different options, including the invasion of Cuba to overthrow Castro's government and take out the missiles, a blockade of the island, using nuclear weapons against Cuba and/or the Soviet Union, or bombing the sites using conventional bombers. Several of the men were having doubts about the wisdom of a bombing raid, fearing that it would lead to a nuclear war with the Soviet Union. The committee discussed these options for the next two days and was now so divided that a firm decision could not be made.

    The CIA and the military were still in favor of a bombing raid and an invasion. However, the majority of the committee gradually began to favor a naval blockade of Cuba. In a televised speech, Kennedy explained to a tense nation and the world why it was necessary to impose a naval blockade on Cuba. Along with a naval blockade, Kennedy also instructed the Air Force to prepare for attacks on Cuba and the Soviet Union. Any missile launch from Cuba would be considered a launch from the Soviet Union, and the world would be at war. The military was also told that if one of the U-2 spy planes were fired upon they were authorized to attack the Cuban surface-to-air (SAM) missile sites.

https://www.youtube.com/watch?v=DpjQDlmGZB0

U-2 spy plane photograph of Soviet missile installations being built in Cuba

The world waited anxiously for the start of World War III, a war that no one could possibly win. In preparation for what appeared to be a major invasion, the De La Cruz and Martínez clan could only watch helplessly as convoys of American troops passed their home in Miami towards Key West. The United States armed forces went to their highest state of readiness, and Soviet field commanders in Cuba were ordered to use whatever means necessary to defend the island if it were invaded. U.S. Army units quickly positioned 125,000 men in Florida and were awaiting orders to invade Cuba. If the Soviet ships carrying weapons for Cuba did not turn back, the orders from Washington were for war.

On October 24, President Kennedy was informed that Soviet ships had stopped just before they reached the blockade line of American ships. Had they crossed the blockade, U.S. Navy ships were authorized to strike.[19] Two days later, Khrushchev sent Kennedy a letter proposing that the Soviet Union would be willing to remove the missiles in Cuba in exchange for a promise by the United States that they would not invade Cuba. To the Kennedys, this meant that if they accepted this agreement, no large scale invasion force, like the one seen during the Bay of Pigs debacle, could be authorized in the future. Low-level guerrilla attempts to start an internal uprising, however, were still possible.

The following day, Washington received a second letter from Khrushchev demanding that the United States remove their nuclear missiles in Turkey. This was clearly a face-saving tactic by Khrushchev necessary for his political cover. While the president and his advisers were analyzing

---

[19] Schlesinger, Arthur M. Jr. 1965, 2002. <u>A Thousand Days: John F. Kennedy in the White House.</u> Houghton Mifflin

Khrushchev's two letters, news arrived at the White House that a U-2 plane had just been shot down over Cuba. The leaders of the military, reminding Kennedy of the rules of engagement he had ordered, argued that the President should immediately authorize the bombing of Cuba. Kennedy refused and instead sent a letter to Khrushchev accepting the terms of his first letter.

http://www.youtube.com/watch?v=Xo8SMzM8X-U

Chapter Five

The Rise of the Mambise Commandos

"Goals without commitment usually fall by the wayside from a lack of interest by its beholder. Only when we fully commit to a dream are we able to access the highest possibilities of our being."
　　　　　　　　　　　　　　　　　　　　　　　Rafael Martínez Púpo

The Cuban Missile Crisis was the first and only nuclear confrontation between the United States and the Soviet Union. The event appeared to frighten both sides, marking a significant change in the development of the Cold War. It led to the establishment of a direct line of communication that became known as the "hot line" and the signing of the Nuclear Test Ban Treaty. Eventually, the crisis would lay the foundations for negotiations to reduce the number of nuclear weapons altogether.

　　　　The nuclear crisis, however, did little to stop the goal to liberate our homeland from a Communist dictatorship. The agreement between the United States and the Soviet Union had been understood by those in the West as preventing only large scale invasions of Cuba. Low-level hit-and-run campaigns continued unabated. Regardless, given this international agreement, there was a level of activity that the CIA and Rafael Martínez Púpo were under orders not to exceed.

Grandfather Rafael, however, was an ambitious and creative entrepreneur. He had never been completely satisfied with the small scale hit and run tactics to harass Castro's government. He considered them petty, an unproductive use of manpower and resources. In this way, he was philosophically and fundamentally in opposition with the wishes of Bobby Kennedy's goals of attacking economic targets in the hope of generating some popular uprising in our homeland. For a while at least, Grandfather Rafael played someone else's game while laying the foundations of his own, bolder international move.

August 18, 1963, Rafael Martinez entered the offices of the Miami Herald in Guatemala City to announce that the new Mambise Commandos had bombed the oil refinery in Casilda, Cuba. He introduced the commandos to the world by stating that with a force of more than one thousand men operating from Central America, the Dominican Republic and from inside Cuba itself, the Mambises were back and ready to again change the course of Cuban history.[20] In reality, the Commandos Mambises numbered fewer than fifty, mostly

---

[20] Rafael Martinez Pupo Papers. University of Florida Collection

2 Small Boats Shell Plant In Cuba Raid

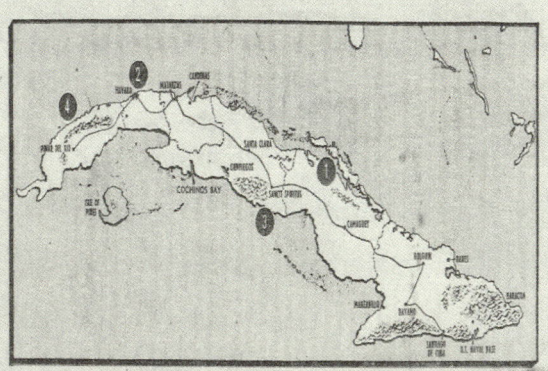

REBEL FORAYS OF THE LAST 72 HOURS: Bombing run on sugar mill at Cunagua (1); abortive flight over Havana (2); bomb hit on oil tank at Casilda (3); and shelling off Santa Lucia (4).

By HAL HENDRIX
Miami News Latin America Editor

The Cuban government angrily charged today that two small "pirate" boats staged a hit-and-run attack with bazookas and machine guns on a north coast industrial plant and inflicted some damage.

No casualties were reported in the attack, the fourth foray by anti-Castro rebels in the last 72 hours.

An official government communique, published and broadcast in Havana, declared:

"We make the United States government directly responsible for this cowardly attack.

"This is the third pirate attack against our country in the last 72 hours, which proves once more that the beginning of a new plan of aggression against Cuba is under way, as announced by the American press." (The Cuban government apparently was ignoring an abortive flight over Havana last weekend.)

The communique stated that the bazooka projectiles fired by the raiders missed their target, but that 30-cal. machine gun bullets punctured oil storage and sulphuric acid tanks as well as some pipelines.

The apparent target was a sulphometal plant on the Santa Lucia estuary, about 100 miles southwest of Havana in Pinar del Rio province.

The government's announcement said the raiders' two small boats crept up the estuary at 1:30 a.m. Monday along a channel which the raiders had previously marked with buoys.

The communique charged that the small craft came from an unidentified mother ship anchored off the coast.

The attackers, according to the government, made their escape under cover of heavy machine gun fire from the mother ship.

Cuban militia, the government said, recovered the buoys, one of the small boats, one outboard motor, an 88.9 mm. bazooka, two 30-cal. machine guns, ammunition, an empty gasoline tank, seven blasting caps and one bazooka projectile.

The communique said ". . . the costly means employed by the aggressor can only be within the reach of the (U.S.) Central Intelligence Agency, which draws up the plans, organizes the bases and supplies the technical resource ansd techniques for

Continued on Page 5A, Col. 2

men without families to miss them. In an unprecedented move, Rafael then announced where the Mambises would attack next. That evening the commandos destroyed an industrial plant on the north coast of the island. They struck at least three more times that year, attacking and damaging a Cuban patrol boat docked at Isabela de Sagua in Las Villas. Each Mambise attack led to spontaneous sabotage events inside the island, giving credence to Bobby Kennedy's goals of inciting internal Cuban resistance, such as the derailment of a train or the hijacking of government truck convoys.

In December of 1963, a Soviet patrol boat stationed on the Isle of Pines was seriously damaged and probably sunk. Rafael Martínez Púpo's communiqué was relayed to the media in Miami through Salvador Lew, an active member of the exile community who had escorted Fidel Castro's sister Juanita Castro when she defected to the United States. In 2001, Mr. Lew would be appointed by President George W. Bush as director of Radio Martí, a U.S. government anti-Castro radio station based on the Voice of America.

Grandfather Rafael would communicate with island agents using "burst" of radio transmissions, messages that were enciphered using a numerical system punched into a paper tape and loaded onto an FSS-7 transmitter. These transmissions were made at an agreed time to a receiver at such a high speed that it could not be picked up by any radio-direction finder. Despite the precautions, there were a few setbacks, convincing Grandfather Rafael Martínez Púpo that low-level tactics were simply not the shock and awe that was necessary to do the job.

One of the missions targeted the giant Matahambre copper mine near Cape Corrientes on the boot heel of Pinar del Río Province. When the Rex arrived at the landing zone, there was a sense of concern that soon confirmed itself to the Mambise command as a trap. The Commando's speedboats took on extensive fire from enemy forces and contact was lost with several members of the team who were quickly taken captive. The missing members of the Mambise Commandos were made prisoner of the Castro regime and brought to "La Baban" Prison to be interrogated.

The mission began on October 21, 1963. The Rex was on a course that would bring it dangerously close to the Cuban shore and within range of coastal defenses. At a designated rendezvous point off the coast of Florida, Captain Brooks ordered the Rex engines to a full stop. Two black rubber rafts appeared; the men in them were dressed in black with black stockings over their faces as they boarded the Rex in silence. There were ten of them, members of the Commandos Mambises. Off Elliot Key, an insignificant speck in the

Caribbean below Miami, the sea was choppy as the Rex throttled back its twin screws. Once boarded, the Rex was suddenly underway, headed towards the Mambises' ultimate target. Arriving off the coast of Cuba, the two fiberglass speedboats again slid down the afterdeck of the mother ship splashing in the water.

The Mambises were proud warriors, their emblem was the Lone Star of Cuba, and they prided themselves with being the elite force of the Secret War to liberate their homeland. Stocking-masked commandos climbed down the side cargo nets of the Rex with their backpacks loaded with C-4 plastic explosives. Grandfather Rafael frequently spoke of the

bravery of these men during all their missions. That evening, their 100-horsepower inboard motors coughed to life, the noise muffled by exhaust deflectors. The double-bottomed boats had been specially designed for the CIA's amphibious operations and had been baptized by the commandos with the name "moppies." They carried two .30-caliber Browning machine guns and a radio to communicate with their mother ship.

It was a moonless night providing an added cover of darkness as the moppies headed toward the mouth of a river bank by the Cuban shore. For the last leg of this journey, they switched to silent-running mode as the commandos quietly made their way up river to meet with two Mambise operatives who had been infiltrated into Cuba a week earlier. The rafts slowed in the river, and the Mambises signaled shore with an infrared blinker. Within minutes the wrong response came back signaling a trap. The commandos scrambled to head back to the moppies using cover fire from their submachine guns. One of the rafts was ripped apart by Cuban gunfire opening up on both banks on the fleeing rafts. The moppies made it out to sea, spilling the dead and dying commandos into the water while the other craft joined in making a getaway. A Cuban patrol boat was in hot pursuit of both Mambise boats as they sped out to international waters. The two abandoned commandos held no hope of escape and turned towards shore where Castro's militia awaited them.

At sea, a fleeing moppie was spotted in the searchlight of the Russian patrol boat and captured, its cargo of elite commandos taken prisoner. The other moppie headed for deep sea and the spot in the night sky where the Rex had been expected, speeding until it reached just beyond Cuban territorial waters. Reaching a well navigated naval corridor heavy with commercial seagoing traffic, the lone moppie stopped a merchant ship by firing his machine gun across its bow, boarding to safety.

The Rex, however, was nowhere in sight. Captain Brooks had seen the firefight through the ships "eyes," high-powered binoculars located in the signal bridge. He had suspected this mission could be a trap. The ambush of the commandos had confirmed his worst fears as he quickly ordered the Rex to depart the area at flank speed, leaving the commandos to fend for themselves.

To a few of the commandos, it was an all too familiar pattern of Americans plans followed by a last minute lack of support. Some were angry and remembered the failure of American support during the Bay of Pigs. Most of the Mambiese, however, understood the decision. The Rex was too valuable an asset to lose to Castro's forces. Minutes after the firefight began on shore, a pair of Cuban helicopters appeared over the scene where the Rex usually waited for the commandos. Cuban intelligence had been good and accurate. The Cuban attack helicopters illuminated the sea with flares as the Rex crew observed from a safe distance. An innocent freighter which happened to be in the vicinity of the Cuban action came into view of the illuminated flares. When the freighter ran into the light of the flares, the Cubans thought they had cornered the Rex and opened fire. This ship, however, was not the Rex; it was the 32,500 ton *J. Louis*,[21] flying the Liberian flag and hauling a cargo of bauxite from Jamaica to Texas.

It was just before 1:00 a.m., as five Cuban Mig-21s equipped for night fighting began strafing runs on the *J. Louis*. Her bewildered skipper, Captain Gerhard Krause, radioed an international SOS call: *"Unarmed freighter under MIG attack off the coast of Cuba."* Fighter air units of the United States scrambled into action. American F-4 Phantom fighter jets out of south Florida were soon screaming towards the site of the attack, forcing the Cubans to withdraw.

At the Cuban prison, far from the battles being raged just off the cost of the island, a dark and damp corridor of stone held some of Grandfather Rafael's brave men. La Baban Prison was an old pile of masonry. The Mambise captives were held in chains inside their cells. In the hot, humid climate of Cuba the interior of the prison was cool, a welcome respite from the heat outside. Yet in the dark corridors filled with stagnant air, the odor of mold and decay seemed almost overpowering. The iron bars, grates and cell doors were wet

---

[21] Rafael Martinez Pupo Papers. University of Florida Collection

with condensation, covered with layers of rust. During the day small windows with nearly opaque, dirty glass admitted what light there was. At night, naked bulbs hung where corridors met, or an iron gate barred the way, lighting the interior. For whole stretches of corridors and dungeon-like cells there was no light at all. Two days passed and on October 23, 1963, Fidel Castro appeared on Havana television to describe the CIA ship the Rex, bringing on stage two of the missing men, Rex Quartermaster Luis Montera Carranzana, who had piloted a moppie, and Dr. Clemente Inclán Werner, a Mambise agent. At the White House press conference, the Kennedys' press secretary Pierre Salinger simply answered "no comment."

Besides the Mambises, there were other CIA-funded exile groups were still active but experiencing mixed results. One was headed by Manuel Artime[22] who had been a captain in the Cuban rebel army against Batista and subsequent commander of the Bay of Pigs Brigade 2506. Working from Nicaragua, Artime was funded by the CIA with $100,000 per month, working with disgruntled Cuban military personnel as a prelude to an anti-Castro coup. The Artime project moved forward and several weapons caches were placed on the island for Artime's people.

---

[22] Bohning, Don (2005). The Castro Obsession: U.S. Covert Operations Against Cuba, 1959–1965. Washington, D.C.: Potomac Books, Inc

In addition, there were several additional plots to assassinate Castro. In 1962 the Cuban Task Force organized three different plots. This included working with a man named Rolando Cubela,[23] a senior official in Castro's government. CIA operatives, however, suspected that Cubela was a double agent recruited by Castro to penetrate the American plots against him. These suspicions were not helped by the fact that Rolando Cubela repeatedly refused to take a lie-detector test, convincing Ted Shackley that he was in fact a double-agent.

Senior members of the CIA met with Cubela in Paris on the 29th of October, 1963, where Cubela requested a high-powered rifle with a silencer in order to kill Fidel Castro. The CIA rejected his request and instead insisted that Rolando Cubela use poison. On the 22nd of November, 1963, the CIA handed over a pen supplied with a hidden syringe. Cubela was told to use a deadly poison favored by the agency called Black Leaf 40 to kill Castro.

Half a world away in Miami, on the exact moment that Cubela was walking out of the meeting with the CIA, I found myself using my parents' bed as a trampoline, bouncing up

---

[23] Campbell, Duncan (April 3, 2006). "638 ways to kill Castro". London: The Guardian Unlimited. Retrieved 2006-05-28

10A THE MIAMI NEWS, Wed., August 21, 1963

Rebel Raiders Say Fidel Isn't Admitting Damage

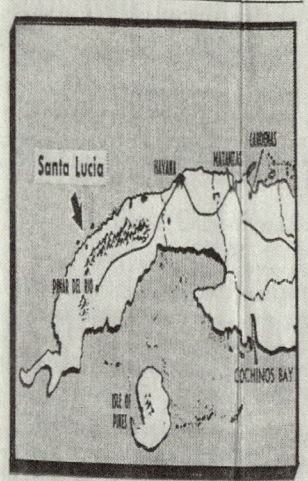

Santa Lucia – How Hard Hit?

Continued from Page 1A Villas Province, warned that more raids are imminent.

Rafael Martinez Pupo, spokesman for the group, said:

"The war of liberation continues. Commandos Mambises have struck again. On the night of Aug. '18, Commandos Mambises attacked the power plant at Santa Lucia in northern Pinar del Rio province.

"The fight for liberty is being waged against Castro and the Communists as they are the true enemies of the oppressed Cuban people.

"Patriots in Cuba must respond to our call to arms. Now is the time to burn, delay, kill, confuse and resist Fidelismo in all its manifestations."

In its official communique yesterday announcing the attack at Santa Lucia, the Castro government said the raiders missed their target but admitted that some damage was done to oil storage and sulphuric acid tanks and pipelines.

Cuban exiles here familiar with the sulphurmetal plant at Santa Lucia and the Matahambre copper mine note that an electrically powered conveyor system moved supplies and copper concentrates between the mine and the port city – a distance of about 14 kilometers.

According to reports, the conveyor system is now inoperative. Also, because of damage inflicted on the power plant, control of water seepage and ventilation into the copper mining area has been lost.

Importance of the Matahambre mines is noted in published statistics of the Cuban Ministry of Finance. Between 1940 and 1958, the mines produced 70 per cent of all copper and copper concentrates exported by Cuba.

and down on the bed. The television in the bedroom proceeded with its programming, ignored by the figure of a six-year-old Cuban boy finding joy in the illicit use of his parents' bed springs to reach the sky. Suddenly, the voice of a man on the television stated in a stern and concerned voice: ***"We interrupt this program for a special bulletin; President Kennedy has just been shot.***" Probably everyone that was alive during that time can clearly remember where they were or what they were doing on that fateful November day in American history. At the exact moment that I froze to the news and stared at the television in shock, Cubela was leaving the CIA meeting in Paris to the same news that President John F. Kennedy had been assassinated. Both Cubela and Artime's projects were subsequently cancelled, as was of course, my attempts to reach the skies.

With the assassination of President Kennedy in Dallas, Texas, Vice President Lyndon Johnson assumed the Presidency of the United States while the Mambise Commandos continued their operations in the Caribbean. The MIG attack on an American ship in international waters was still fresh in everyone's mind, but Grandfather Rafael needed reassurance that the new American Administration would continue its support for military action against Castro's Cuba.

Rafael wrote a letter to President Johnson appealing to him to continue the struggle against Cuban communism. His aim was to gain a sense of reassurance that the cause to bring freedom to his island had not died with Kennedy.

> Mr. Lindon B. Johnson.
> Honorable Presidente de los Estados
> Unidos de Norte-America.
> La casa Blanca, Washington.
> U.S.A.
>
> Honorable Señor Presidente-
>
> Unidades navales de vuestro pais, han sido atacadas por unidades de un pais pirata.- Los antiguos piratas asaltaban, robaban y arrasaban ciudades, hasta que los paises demócratas procedieron a su exterminio.
>
> Los actuales piratas denominados comunistas, asaltan-hoy a paises felices y laboriosos robando sus libertades, robando sus riquezas y sumiendo a sus habitantes en el hambre, en el terror, en la esclavidud y muerte.
>
> Al mismo tiempo que lo felicito Honorable Sr. Presidente por sus decisión ordenando repelir esos ataques, le brindo mi modesta cooperación, y no tengo ninguna duda que las mismas están respaldadas por todos los habitantes del mundo que desean vivir libres y le digo de todo el mundo sin señalar solo a los paises democráticos, porque no podemos desconocer que en esos paises piratas-comunistas, viven centenares centenares de miles de seres con la vista puesta en nosotros, clamando libertad.
>
> FE en DIOS, Honorable Señor Presidente, y prosigamos adelante; tenemos que vivir y si llega el caso también morir, con dignidad, con decoro.
>
> Respetuosamente de Vd.,
>
> Rafael Martinez Pupo.

1963 Letter from Rafael Martínez Púpo to the President of the United States, Lyndon B. Johnson referencing the attack on the American freighter J. Luis and encouraging him to continue the struggle against Castro.

Translation:

Mr. Lyndon B. Johnson
Honorable President of the United States
of North America
The White House, Washington
U.S.A

Honorable Mr. President

    Naval units of your nation have been attacked by naval forces of a pirate nation. Throughout history, pirates have assaulted, robbed and pillaged cities until democratic nations found the resolve to exterminate them.
    The current Communist pirates are today attacking freedom loving nations robbing them of liberty, taking their riches and submitting their inhabitants in the name of terror to slavery or death.
    At the same time that I congratulate you Mr. President, for your decision to order the repelling of these pirate attacks, I offer to you sir, my modest cooperation. I know that your decisions are fully supported by all the inhabitants of nations that desire to live free, and I can honestly tell you from all nations without signaling out just the democratic nations, knowing that even within those Communist nations there live tens of thousands of human beings that hold our point of view, yearning to be free.
    Have faith in God, Honorable Mr. President, and let us proceed ahead; we must continue to pursue life, but should it be the case that we should die, let us do so with dignity.

        Very Respectfully,

            Rafael Martínez Púpo

Inside Havana's revolutionary circles, the Mambise Commando raids were increasingly being felt. Castro began to use all his influence to pressure Latin American nations to close down the Mambises' stations. But Rafael and the CIA network remained one step ahead. Rafael Martínez Púpo traveled extensively and continuously all over Latin America, countering all efforts of Castro's agents to shut down his network of warriors.

In Miami, the family waited anxiously for any news of the war and the whereabouts of Grandfather Rafael. As a family we never really knew when he would show up at our front door, and it wasn't unusual for a knock at the door in the early evening to reveal the unexpected silhouette of a man wearing a fedora hat, like some scene from a Hollywood movie. No sooner had he arrived than he would be gone again and the waiting game would begin anew.

On the home front, my father Eduardo had left the A&P store, taking a job as a salesman with Carnation Company, a multinational corporation during that time in history with headquarters in Los Angeles, California. His contacts with the Cuban exile community and the salesman abilities developed over time in Havana before the revolution made him a noticeable asset for the company.

8A THE MIAMI NEWS, Thursday, August 22, 1963

Guatemalans Gag Voice Of Cuba Raiders

By HAL HENDRIX
Miami News Latin America Editor

The Guatemalan government has ordered the Cuban exile spokesman for Commandos Mambises in Guatemala City to stop issuing communiques on hit-and-run attacks against Cuba, The Miami News learned today.

Rafael Martinez Pupo, who earlier this week identified himself as the spokesman for anti-Castro raider bands which struck at La Casilda and Santa Lucia in Cuba, was summoned to the national palace in the Guatemalan capital yesterday afternoon.

According to reports from Guatemala City, Rafael Escobar Arguello, secretary of information for the presidency, notified Martinez Pupo that the government would not permit him to make statements "which could jeopardize the peace and tranquility of Guatemala."

The Guatemalan press secretary told the Mambises spokesman that Guatemala would honor all its international commitments and would take part in any action supported by all Latin American nations against Cuba.

By the same token, the Guatemalan official added, Guatemala could not allow "the impression to be created that it was allowing isolated attacks to take place against Cuba."

Martinez Pupo explained that he was serving only as a spokesman for Commandos Mambises, and that it should be obvious to the Guatemalan officials that his organization's attacks were coming from areas other than Guatemala.

At the request of the press secretary, Martinez Pupo then agreed not to make any further announcements from Guatemala City about the operations.

Early yesterday he issued a statement in Guatemala City, saying that the Commandos Mambises had attacked Santa Lucia in Cuba's Pinar del Rio province and urged Cuban patriots in Cuba to "burn, kill, delay, confuse and resist Fidelismo in all its manifestations."

Britain: Return 19 Exiles

Continued from Page 1A

the note at length before offering a reply," Scott said.

In its note, the British referred to assurances given Castro in April that Britain was not going to allow its nearby island territories to be used as jumping-off spots for illegal activities against the Cuban regime.

In Miami, British Consul Frank Smitherman said that routine diplomatic procedure would be for the Cuban government to deliver its reply to Scott in Havana, who would, in turn, relay it to London.

The protest, in part, stated:

"Her Majesty's Government therefore protests vigorously against this incursion into Brit-

Guatemalan Government reacts to Cuban pressure attempts to silence Grandfather Rafael Martínez Púpo

The experience my father had gained in Havana working with Grandfather Rafael Martínez Púpo's sales force now began to bear some fruit for the family. Eduardo had been selected out of a pool of several hundred to become a sales representative in the Miami area catering to the myriad of small Latin markets that were sprouting all over South Florida. The effects of this career change allowed us to move away from that dilapidated old shack that was our home, moving into a new development in Hialeah, Florida.

Our new three bedroom home was across the street from a man-made lake, a lake which for me possessed the best of what my imagination required. A small island at the center of the lake became the primary objective for both my friend Wayne and me to conquer. We immediately set out to build a raft to "sail the seas" to what in reality amounted to little more than a sand bar not more than five or six feet in diameter, but to us, the island was mysterious and magical. We yearned to discover the quicksand that we were sure existed in the center of this "island." While we plotted our strategy, we gathered wood debris and anything that we thought would float for the grand raft that would take us on our journey.

When Wayne and I weren't planning our voyage, we enjoyed endless hours of fishing at the lake. I was a still a crew-cut southern boy who had learned to run on the rocky shores of this lake without any shoes, never feeling the jagged edges of the multitudes of pebbles and rocks along the way.

Former Cuban Ambassador Eduardo Carlos De La Cruz selling Carnation Evaporated Milk to Cuban owned small stores in Miami

Though fishing was a leisurely act, my parents considered the lake a source of great concern for me. I was never really allowed to pursue my constant need to observe the island by the shores of the lake while waiting for that fish to take the bait, bait which undoubtedly consisted of a spitball of bread tightly packed into a marble and hooked at the end of my fishing line. I would frequently sneak out of the house with my fishing pole leaning against my shoulder, making my way to the side of our home and proceeding down to the lake.

It was a constant cat and mouse game with my mother who clearly held the magical ability to spot me no matter how hard I tried to conceal my flight. My attempts to get from our home to the lake were almost always foiled by my mother calling my name out of nowhere, demanding that I return to the house. Only years later did I realize that she could see my fishing pole bobbing up and down past the kitchen window on my way to my favorite fishing site. As a child, I was oblivious to the dangerous waters that really did exist outside my private little world. What I did know was that my grandfather had his island to conquer, while at the same time that I had mine.

On the war front, the CIA over time had been gradually losing control over Grandfather Rafael as the leadership of the Mambise exerted more independence from the Agency and moved more towards an effort to overthrow rather than simply harass Castro's regime. It was clear that some elements of the otherwise disciplined Commandos, including Grandfather Rafael, were showing signs of going rogue.

Chapter Six

The "Rafael Plan"

The whole course of human history may depend on a change of heart in one solitary and even humble individual - for it is in the solitary mind and soul of the individual that the battle between good and evil is waged and ultimately won or lost.

M. Scott Peck

By the middle of 1962, Rafael had begun to produce concrete results in the establishment of an international network of Cuban exiles and former Cuban politicians. A government in exile was beginning to take shape independent of CIA influence. Guillermo Alonso Pujol, the former Vice President of Cuba, and uncle of my father's sister-in-law, had accepted Rafael's invitation to assume the role of provisional President of Cuba with Castro's downfall.[24] The former Vice President would provide the familiar face necessary for legitimacy of the provisional government, and Pujol had agreed to hold this temporary position until internationally supervised elections could take place. In the meantime, the

---

[24] A Guide to the Rafael Martínez Pupo Papers Relating to Comandos Mambises. Finding aid created by Margarita Vargas-Betancourt. University of Florida Smathers Libraries - Special and Area Studies Collections. November 2011

former Vice President was campaigning to gather $100,000 dollars in order to pay the demands of Fidel Castro's government for the release of his son, a private in the Cuban exile force that had landed at the Bay of Pigs. He would eventually succeed in flying to Havana with cash in hand to purchase his son's freedom.

Former Cuban Vice President Guillermo Alonso Pujol (left) with Former Cuban President Carlos Prío Socarras (right), who would shoot himself in 1977, the day before being questioned by the Select Committee on Assassination of JFK

Rafael's intensive travels throughout Latin America provided the CIA with the ability to widely disseminate information on Mambise Commando strikes against the Castro Regime. Those frequent travels also enabled the agency the ability to claim the Mambise network was larger and more widespread than it actually was. For the moment at least, their image was much larger than their reality, and this disturbed Grandfather Rafael who held on to his own greater visions for liberating Cuba. He had been a loyal soldier for the CIA, going along with the small-scale guerrilla tactics dictated by Bobby Kennedy, aiming at low-level economic targets around the island. In Rafael's mind at least, all this was about to change.

With the CIA acting as facilitators, Rafael Martínez Púpo was sent on a clandestine mission to meet with the President of the Dominican Republic, Juan Bosch. His mission was to secure bases of operations for the Mambise force on that adjacent nation. Other bases of operation were set up in the Central American nation of Guatemala with a few small scale supply points within Cuba itself manned by the Cuban underground. What was missing for the entrepreneurial Rafael was coordinated military action on a grander scale. This is where the French Foreign Legion, stationed in the North African French colony of Algeria, became of interest to him.

With the Algerian independence of July 1962, several thousand highly trained French Foreign Legionnaires had become obsolete. The Legion was a separate and unique unit of the regular French Army created as a unit of foreign volunteers but commanded by French officers. They were principally used to protect and expand the French colonial empire. These Legionnaires were elite military units whose training was a superb example of physical, psychological and military challenges. With an exceptional sense of unity and discipline, they had been heavily engaged in fighting against the Algerian National Liberation Front from 1954 to 1962.

The government of France had no intentions of disbanding the Legionnaires with the looming Algerian independence, but their numbers were more than would be needed to be maintained on the payroll. As a result, by 1962, several thousand legionnaires were on the verge of finding themselves out of a job. Grandfather Rafael Martínez Púpo used all his connections to immediately secure an audience with Spanish General Francisco Franco, the hard-line Spanish dictator, with a plan to secure these "retiring" troops for what would become a second ground invasion of Cuba.

Mr. José León, from the city of Tenerife in the Canary Islands, a Cuban exile member of the Catholic organization of Opus Dei, was made an honorary member of the Mambise Commandos. In late 1963 he sent a letter to Grandfather Rafael to cryptically inform him that he had *"exchanged ideas (on the plan) with friends (in Spain) and they were willing to enthusiastically collaborate.*"[25] He also introduced Rafael Martínez Púpo to a well-connected Cuban expatriate named Don Oscar Garcia Celhay who was also active with Opus Dei. Mr. Celhay was willing to connect the Mambise leadership within a few days with "friends in Madrid."

One cannot stress enough the importance of the role played by the Opus Dei organization in Rafael's plans. Opus Dei is a controversial force within the Catholic Church that was founded in Spain in the late 1920's by a Roman Catholic priest. The organization was instrumental in assisting General Francisco Franco gain power during the Spanish Civil War in 1936. Some would say they were the key player in placing General Franco in power. The society has been linked to right-leaning political activities due to the politics of most of its members. During the Cold War, Opus Dei was viewed as a powerful force to combat the spread of a Communist philosophy of atheism as one of its primary tenets, while at the same time spreading Catholic doctrine. The organization was more than willing to assist Grandfather Rafael in this shared goal. This became a key factor in Rafael's ability to reach General Franco through the back channels of its secretive organization. General Franco was Opus Dei, and so were

---

[25] A Guide to the Rafael Martínez Pupo Papers Relating to Comandos Mambises. Finding aid created by Margarita Vargas-Betancourt. University of Florida Smathers Libraries - November 2011

Cuban exiles in Spain that were members of the Mambise Commando force.

  The Spanish Dictator's role was also instrumental for the plan to work. The General had assumed power with his victory during the 1936 Spanish Civil War. The result of the Spanish Civil War would have a direct and indirect impact on the De La Cruz and Martinez family in the early 1960's. It was a Spanish refugee from the losing side of that Civil War, an employee of my Grandfather Rafael in Cuba, who would denounce my father to the Castro authorities, leading to the acceleration of our defection plans to the United States. In 1963, the victor of that Civil War would now assist the Mambise Commandos and my grandfather with his plans to retake Cuba from Castro's Communist control.

  There was a very strong connection between General Franco and the French Foreign Legion. The General had been commander of the Spanish Foreign Legion in North Africa, a force that was modeled after the French Legion. The Generalissimo was particularly fond of the Legions. Back in the 1920's he was the newly founded Spanish Foreign Legion's second in command. Under Franco, the Spanish Foreign Legion had saved the Spanish enclave in North Africa after a grueling three-day forced march so that by 1923, Franco was named commander of the Spanish Legion. It was clear to all that the code of the Legionnaires was buried deep within the dictator's heart.

During the Algerian war for independence, Madrid had been the headquarters of the French "Secret Army Organization," the OAS, a right-wing French Army group which was focused on preserving Algeria as an integral part of greater France.[26] While Spain was supporting the French Legionnaires in Algeria, it was also refusing to respect the American-imposed 1962 economic embargo on Castro's Cuba. Washington had threatened Spain with the withdrawal of American aid as a result of that refusal and Spanish ships were also being attacked by anti-Castro groups funded by the CIA for defying the embargo. Several Spanish sailors had already been killed.

The CIA initially sent Grandfather Rafael to confer with General Franco in an attempt to repair relations between Spain and the anti-Castro groups. He was to advise the General that Franco's Spain would obtain greater influence in Cuba after the defeat of Castro. But Rafael went beyond the charter provided to him.

From the CIA's perspective, repairing relations was the extent of Rafael's mission but Grandfather Rafael had

---

[26] Harrison, Alexander (1989). <u>Challenging De Gaulle: The OAS and the counterrevolution in Algeria (1954-1962)</u>. Greenwood press

other ideas in mind. In addition to completing his orders for the CIA, Rafael was acting on a letter he had received on the 14th of February 1964, from his designated provisional Cuban President Alonso Pujol. In this letter, a copy of which is now with the University of Florida achieves on the Mambise Commandos, Pujol informed Rafael Martínez Púpo that he had "accomplished his goals in Spain, making the Spanish government aware of his "enterprise."[27]

Shortly after receiving this letter, Rafael met with General Franco and laid out his plans for the second invasion of Cuba, an invasion plan that would defy the Kennedy-Khrushchev agreement and the American promise never to again invade the island. The plan became known as the "Rafael Plan." It is a plan that has never been recorded in history.

Rafael understood that there was a direct connection between the Algerian War of Independence and the struggle against Fidel Castro's Cuba. The Algerian independence movement began in 1954 when Cuba was under the dictatorship of Batista. From November of 1954, the Algerian rebels united under the banner of the National Liberation Front and began actively conducting guerilla warfare against the French Army. The independence struggle led to acts of

---

[27] Rafael Martinez Pupo Papers. University of Florida Collection

terrorism against civilians and the use of torture on both sides of the conflict which eventually grew to a full-scale war. This would become a war that would shake the very foundations of the French Republic as the French began a campaign of pacification of what was considered at the time to be part of France.

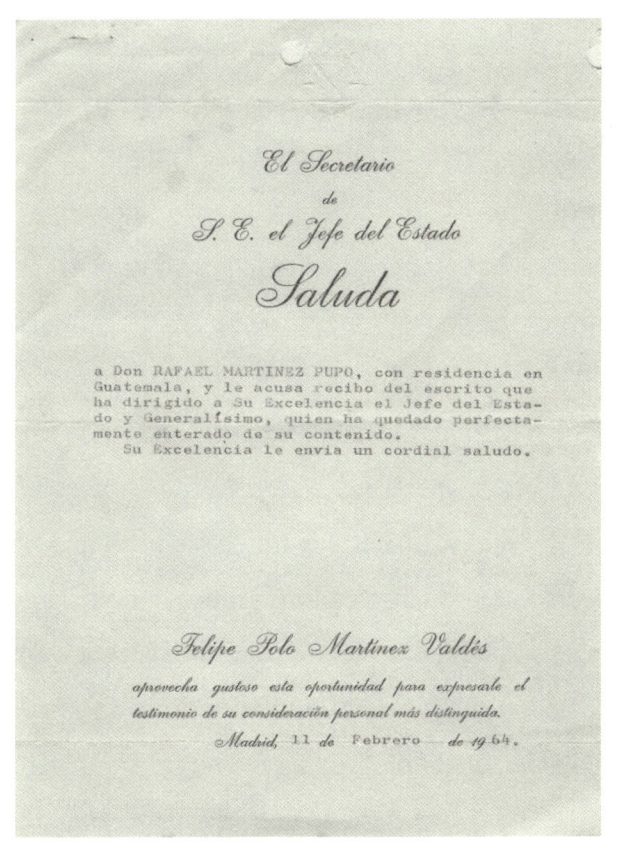

TRANSLATION: "The Secretary for the Head of State, Welcomes Don Rafael Martínez Púpo, with residence in Guatemala, and acknowledges receipt of his letter directed to his Excellency the Head of State and Generalissimo, who has been made fully aware of its contents. His Excellency sends his most cordial regards." Felipe Polo Martínez Valdes, (brother-in-law of General Francisco Franco), 11 March, 1964.

In 1957, the year I was born, the commander of the French Army had divided the Algerian colony into defensive sectors in an attempt to suppress the independence-seeking rebels. These methods sharply reduced the rebel terrorism, but tied down large numbers of French forces in stationary defensive positions throughout the colony. Rebels were infiltrating from Tunisia and Morocco, while the French army ruthlessly applied the same tactics used by Spanish General Weyler in Cuba during the Cuban war for independence. A program was initiated by the French to concentrate large segments of the population into camps under military supervision in an attempt to prevent the rural population from aiding the rebellion. More than two million Algerians were removed from their villages. As in Cuba, living conditions became abysmal with entire families scattered and lost. Half a century had passed between the Spanish concentration camps of the Cuban population and the experiences confronting the Algerian people. A sense of solidarity immediately existed between elements of the Cuban revolutionary movement struggling at the time to seize power in Cuba and the rebels in Algeria.

In Paris the French were beginning to fear another humiliating defeat at the hands of a rebellion like the one that had occurred in Vietnam. It was under these circumstances that Charles de Gaulle was returned to power in 1958 as the only public figure capable of rallying an increasingly demoralized nation and giving direction to the French government.

In Cuba, meanwhile, Castro's rebels were closing in from every direction towards Havana. Within the year, Castro would take power from Batista. In contrast to Cuba, by late 1958, the French army had essentially won military control of Algeria and was the closest it would be to victory. But French political developments overtook the French army successes. Opposition to the conflict was growing in France, and pressure was building in the international community for France to grant independence to Algeria.

General Charles de Gaulle, a French nationalist leader of World War II fame, returned to power as President of France with the hope of ensuring Algeria's continued occupation and integration with the French Republic. But instead of pursuing this goal, President de Gaulle progressively shifted his sympathies in favor of Algerian independence. He organized a referendum for the Algerian people to decide their own destiny, with the resulting vote demonstrating a strong desire for independence.

The results of the referendum led France to negotiate a peace accord with the Algerian National Liberation Army in March of 1962 which history remembers as the *Evian* accords. Opposition to these accords soon materialized in the form of French military officers conspiring to form the "Secret Army Organization" (OAS) with headquarters in Franco's Spain. The underground OAS organization immediately initiated a campaign of bombings and nationalistic demonstrations throughout Algeria in order to block the implementation of the accords.

By late 1959, as Fidel Castro solidified his hold on Havana, de Gaulle dramatically reversed his stand on Algeria. In a September 1959 broadcast to the citizens of France, de Gaulle spoke of "self-determination" for Algeria.[28] French extremists began to organize themselves for action against de Gaulle himself. The French President was about to sit down to talk with the very rebels the French army had fought against for more than six years. The de Gaulle presidency now seemed ready to hand over an independent and prosperous Algeria to this rebel army. Colonialists claimed de Gaulle had betrayed them, and with the backing of elements of the French Army, staged an insurrection in January 1960 and again in April of 1961.

---

[28] Diamond, Robert (1970). France under De Gaulle.

The opposition to the French President quickly became extreme. In October of 1960, retired French army general Salan declared total war on de Gaulle. Other generals soon followed. They saw de Gaulle's support for the rebels as a betrayal of all they had fought to achieve in Algeria, especially since the French had essentially won the war.

French Generals Salan, Challe, Zeller, and Jouhaud during the open rebellion against Paris over Algeria, April 1961.

In April of 1961, a second revolt by the French Army in France began. Generals and many senior officers conspired to mutiny and seize control of Algeria from France as a first step in the overthrow of the Paris government. In the first hours of the uprising it was obvious that the de Gaulle government was not sure of its Army's loyalty, not only in Algeria, but also in NATO bases in Western Germany, and even of the officers commanding the garrisons in France. Three paratroop regiments had declared themselves in control of all power of government in defiance of Charles de Gaulle.

Leaders of the coup were identified as four retired French generals, headed by former Chief of the Air Force General Maurice Challe. Tanks began to roll in the streets of Paris as a precaution from airborne troops from Algeria. In fact, two French paratrooper regiments were already waiting in the woods just outside of Paris for Algerian reinforcements that never came. A stern and outraged De Gaulle moved quickly to contain the insurrection with radio broadcast. De Gaulle's pleas for loyalty from the French people extinguished all popular support for the insurrection and a coup in France was averted.

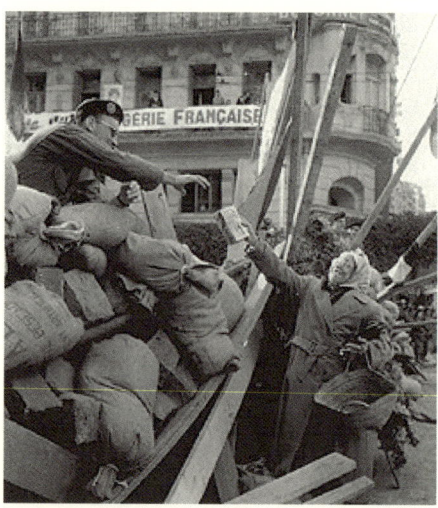

Battle for Paris during the Algerian-related coup attempt

Confrontation in Paris
http://www.youtube.com/watch?v=vJINMsN_5nM&feature=related

    The French people rallied to de Gaulle in a display of national unity and the coup collapsed, but the surviving French army extremists still had their own terrorist group in the form of the Secret Army Organization, which had established a foothold in Franco's Spain under his protection. In this way, General Franco of Spain came to become intimately involved with the French situation in the support of his brethren of French Foreign Legionaries. The OAS launched several attempts on de Gaulle's life as depicted in the book by Frederick Forsyth, *The Day of the Jackal*, but made no headway in their cause as Spain's General Franco continued to gain influence over this elite force.

    It was under this umbrella of confusion and charged emotions that Grandfather Rafael Martínez Púpo entered the fray. His aim was to initially negotiate with the disaffected

French forces to assist his Commandos as far back as late 1962, while the CIA was concentrating on simple harassment tactics on Castro's Cuba. Rafael's motivation to even consider the French troops in Algeria began with the support Castro had given to the Algerian rebel movement. In this international chess game that characterized the Cold War, every move by Castro necessarily precipitated a counter move by the opposing side. Castro had been a full supporter of the Algerian rebel movement in more than just moral support. In the early days of Algerian independence, Castro had dispatched Cuban troops along with armored forces to Algeria to support the new Algerian government of President Ahmed Ben Bella against a counter offensive incursion from Morocco. Rafael saw this situation as an opportunity to tap into the anti-Castro sentiment among the French military.[29]

    With President Ahmed Ben Bella coming to power with the French declaration of Algerian independence on July 3rd, 1962, he never forgot the assistance he received from Castro. In late 1962, resisting pressure from the United States, Ben Bella returned the favor by visiting Cuba. A strong bond developed between the two leaders and President Bella was

---

[29]Heggoy, A.A. (1970), "Colonial origins of the Algerian-Moroccan border conflict of October 1963", African Studies Review

rewarded with a large contingent of Cuban doctors being dispatched to Algeria by Castro.

The Mambise Intelligence network of Cuban exiles had been monitoring Cuban involvement in Algeria with the Moroccan invasion of that newly independent nation. Mambise Commando teams had repeatedly notified Washington through their CIA office in New Orleans that Cuba was taking an active role in the Algerian movement, both pre and post independence. It was their opinion that this represented an expansion of the world Communist march towards world domination.

It was an active role the Cubans themselves freely admitted. One Cuban volunteer in Algeria commented in an interview about Castro's involvement:

> 'The Algerians really reminded us of ourselves in 1959. One had a rifle; another had a shotgun, another, a machine gun, and so on. It was as if we were back in the days of our own Rebel Army in 1959.'[30]

The leader of the Cuban detachment was Colonel Efigenio Ameijeiras, a highly respected Cuban officer of the Castro regime. He commented that,

> 'The orders I had from Fidel were to place myself at their (the Algerian's) complete disposal, to go wherever they wanted whenever they wanted.'

---

[30] How Cuba aided revolutionary Algeria in 1963 – themilitant.com

With those orders, twenty-two T-34 tanks, an artillery group with eighteen 122mm guns, eighteen 120mm mortars and anti-aircraft artillery disembarked from two Cuban freighters. Colonel Amerijeiras continued,

> 'We disembarked dressed in Algerian uniforms, but then we ran out of uniforms, and the rest of us wore civilian clothes. Imagine the racket in Oran, lowering tanks with cranes, and then driving them through the city to the railroad station, where they were loaded on trains to Sidi Bel Abbés in broad daylight! Mers-el-Kébir towered above us and we drove past armored personnel carriers with French paratroopers. There was no way to keep our arrival secret.'[31]

Mambise agents from the Spanish Canary Islands thus began to tap their contacts with the Spanish government of General Franco with the aim of gaining an audience with the Generalissimo himself. Shortly thereafter, the audience with Rafael Martínez Púpo and the Spanish leader soon took place in Madrid's Presidential Palace.

At the Presidential Palace, Rafael Martínez Púpo requested assistance from the Spanish dictator in securing disaffected French Foreign Legionnaires to join the Mambise Commandos in order to attack the Cuban nation. He had successfully argued that Castro's support of the Algerian rebel

---

[31] How Cuba aided revolutionary Algeria in 1963 – themilitant.com

movement had significantly contributed to the humiliating defeat of the French Legion's cause. In addition, Spain was promised a greater role with a free Cuba along with favorable trade agreements with the former colony post-Castro. For their part, Spain would provide the transport ships to deliver the French troops to the landing sites in Cuba.

    Soon after their meeting, word reached Rafael that Spain had secured a commitment of almost 10,000 highly trained Foreign Legionnaires for the second invasion of Cuba. The plans were for 3,000 troops to land at the original Cuban exile invasion site of Trinidad and establish a provisional government under President Pujol which would request world recognition.[32] As Cuban forces were drawn toward the initial landing site of Trinidad, the main invasion force would land on the north shore of Pinar del Río province, just west of San Antonio de los Baños. Paratroopers would secure the José Martí International airport as 7,000 crack troops made their way to take Havana. The psychological impact of losing Havana would demoralize any pro-Castro army elements and entice an expected uprising by the population. The bulk of the Cuban army now focused on Trinidad, would be forced to battle two fronts at once.

---

[32] Interview with Cuban Ambassador Eduardo C. delaCruz

In Trinidad, the provisional Cuban government of President Pujol would request American intervention with U.S. Marines from the Guantánamo base marching onto Santiago de Cuba. The involvement of Spanish naval forces and French troops would have provided an international coalition flavor to this invasion, protecting the image-conscious politicians in Washington and allowing American forces to join the coalition. The Mambise aim was to prevent any repeat of the critical indecisions experienced by the late President John F. Kennedy.

In the comfort of my world in Florida As I learned about history and heard the stories of my Grandfather's exploits as a young boy in Miami, it was as if I was aware of history swirling by, even though I did not fully understand its meaning. It was clear to me even in the early 1960's, however, that our lives had an intrinsic purpose. I was convinced that our existence at that moment in time had to be orchestrated by an intelligence that somehow worked through perfect synchronization to bring about our progression according to a grander plan. It wasn't fate, as people would call it, for fate precluded the existence of free will, and I was sure my will was free. Despite this, I couldn't help but sense that as a people we were required to play within a set of parameters where we existed, confined to wait until something else revealed itself, to finally release us to venture beyond.

While Grandfather Rafael contemplated taking the world into war, in the relative tranquility of Miami, my sister Liz and I enjoyed exploring our childhood. We reveled in the complicated simplicity of the 1960's, confronting the harsh realities of world politics as we learned to lose ourselves in our childhood innocence. In our exiled community, Eduardo was busy exalting the benefits of Carnation evaporated milk to the Cuban merchants in Florida, rebuilding a sense of identity, while members of the extended family opened their own small business enterprises throughout the area. Octavio Buigas, the architect and general contractor nephew of my father had established the *South West Group*, a construction business that would see him build some of the most exquisite buildings and hotels in Florida and Puerto Rico, making him a millionaire several times over.

My father's brother, Carlos Eduardo De La Cruz y Mesa, had moved with his wife, María Teresa Pujol, the niece of the would-be provisional president of a free Cuba, to a teaching position at a Catholic University in Mobile, Alabama. His oldest son and heir to the title of Count of El Castillo had entered the seminary and would eventually become a Jesuit priest. In a compromise with his wife, rather than call his second-born the traditional Eduardo Carlos De La Cruz, he named his youngest son Enrique, after María Teresa's father. Tragedy would strike on Christmas day as their youngest son would be killed leaving midnight mass in 1966 by a drunk driver going the wrong way. "Enriquito," as he was called, would be launched from the back seat of the car by the impact of the on-coming vehicle and would die encrusted in the windshield.

As for me, when I was not fishing at the lake across the street from our home, ever the explorer, I was following the tributaries that led from the lake to the Everglades. In addition, my sister and I, along with my friend Wayne, would ride our bikes in the neighborhood, and it was clear to us at least, that the world was indeed our playground. The prefabricated roofs of the homes yet to be constructed would lie on their side creating a natural bike ramp that led up to the sky for about twenty-five feet or so. Riding to the top of the ramp, our combined weight would slowly roll the upright edge of the roof down until it hit the ground, providing us a means to ride on through. Back and forth we rode our bikes on our own giant see-saw, up and down for hours. While we played, countless thousands of our generations were just buying time, making our way in life preparing to join some greater destiny, even if that destiny was to do battle within ourselves.

In a greater field of battle, another bitter end was taking shape for Grandfather Rafael Martínez Púpo. He had placed his chess pieces for a final move against his arch enemy Fidel Castro. An alliance between his Mambise Commando network and Opus Dei had led to the commitment of an invasion force of 10,000 French Legionnaire troops, convinced the Spanish ruler Franco to provide the logistics and the transportation, and commissioned the invasion plan for a decisive blow against Fidel Castro. All that remained for the plan to be placed in motion was the necessary approvals of the Central Intelligence Agency and the Johnson Administration.

The Rafael plan still lacked an agreement by the presidency of Lyndon Johnson to bankroll the operation, legitimize the Cuban provisional government of Guillermo Pujol, and provide a commitment for Marines to join the liberation struggle when asked to do so. Rafael presented his plan to Ted Shackley at the Roosevelt Hotel in New Orleans in the spring of 1964, and the CIA was immediately aghast[33]. In an unexpected move, on April 7th, 1964, Washington officially brought an end to the sabotage operations against

---

[33] A Guide to the Rafael Martínez Pupo Papers Relating to Comandos Mambises. Finding aid created by Margarita Vargas-Betancourt. University of Florida Smathers Libraries - <u>Special and Area Studies Collections</u>. November 2011

Cuba. John McCone, director of the CIA, stated that President Lyndon B. Johnson had become extremely concerned that the Cuban exile commando groups in general and the Mambise Commandos in particular could not be controlled. The actions of Rafael Martínez Púpo and the Mambises held the real possibility of someday involving America in a World War with the Soviet Union. Washington was shocked not only by the magnitude of the invasion plan, but by the sophistication of the network created to achieve its goal.

The Johnson Administration did briefly debate the Rafael plan, but the prospects of derailing the Kennedy-Khrushchev agreement leading to another superpower confrontation could not have come at a worse time for the United States government. By 1964, the Johnson Administration had decided to escalate the American involvement in the Vietnam War to contain communism in that far off region of the world. It would have been unwise to involve itself in a more direct confrontation with the Soviet Union over an island whose impact on the western hemisphere was perceived by Washington at least, to be under control.

In retrospect, as history would later reveal, had we followed through with this second invasion of Cuba, it would have led to nuclear disaster. In a review of the Cuban Missile Crises held during the 40th anniversary of that crisis, the surviving players gathered in Havana to discuss the details of those fateful thirteen days when the world came close to total destruction. It was learned that despite the Soviet withdrawal of intermediate range nuclear ballistic missiles from Cuba, the Soviet Army had kept tactical nuclear weapons on the island that would have destroyed any major landing force such as that planned by the Mambise Commandos and the French Foreign Legionaries.[34] Given the speed at which the Rafael plan was killed by the Johnson administration, it is likely that Washington may have been privy to the presence of these weapons, leading to the abandonment of the goal to overthrow the Castro regime and sealing the fate of millions of Cubans that were yearning to return home free.

---

[34] 40 Years After Missile Crisis, Players Swap Stories in Cuba. By Kevin Sullivan, Washington Post Foreign Service. Sunday, October 13, 2002

Chapter Seven

America Fights the War Within.

"I am a reliable witness to my own existence. When we look at life through the lens of our potential, we realize the urgency of our purpose"

http://www.youtube.com/watch?v=ClBdf0d0Qc4&feature=related

It was difficult for Rafael to come to terms with the fact that his war was over. The end of the Mambise Commando's goal of returning to a free and liberated Cuba devastated Grandfather Rafael for the second time in his life. He had always been a man of decisive action, from his early days as a fourteen year old boy leaving school to work the farm and deliver milk to the town in support of his family, to the creation of a multimillion dollar empire. He was goal oriented, and while some would have called him a stubborn fool, he succeeded more often than not in achieving what he intended, leading even those who may have thought him a fool to admire his iron will. What became clear is that Rafael Martínez Púpo first had to learn to be in touch with his own sense of power in order to discover his highest possibilities.

Fidel Castro had confiscated his work in Cuba, and now Washington had taken away his dreams of returning in triumph. There is no doubt in my mind, at least, that had he been given the green light by the Johnson Administration, he would have succeeded beyond everyone's expectations, probably even his own. Rafael was a strong believer in God and as such, he attributed any disappointment in his life as God's will. He never thought for a moment that God could mean for him to suffer or be punished in any way. From his point of view, God sometimes acted clumsily, and he often found it hard to see why God had made so many damn fools and democrats. But still, he lived fully, with a deep sense of inner meaning and satisfaction gained from total self-awareness of who he was.

    He felt the loss of his war deeply, but I believe he was able to find some semblance of peace. While he never fully forgave those that had harmed him, in the end he was able to forgive himself and in doing so, to forgive others. There had always been a part of him, a secret sector of his heart that blamed himself for the loss of Cuba and what he had built there, a misstep, a wrong decision, what if he had not sent the convoys of aid to Castro's hideout?

    The void that remained after the quest to regain Cuba was quickly and eagerly filled by the love of his family. No longer would there be prolonged absences to travel the globe under the shadows of the CIA and preach words of war. He and Grandmother Georgina retired quietly to Guatemala City to live in peace. My parents and sister I would visit them frequently over the years, and as a university student, I would often spend my summers staying at their home in Central America and pursuing my own archeological interests in the jungles of Guatemala, working on a University sponsored project on the ancient Mayan city of Tikal.

Rafael's FM radio station, "Intercommunicadora Electrónica," was working well for them in Guatemala as Grandfather Rafael's anchor business. With this station he would transmit music to banks and businesses over leased speakers. In addition, he had the distribution of Texaco gas in the Guatemalan capital city, providing gas cylinders to homes for cooking and heating. Rafael and Georgina also opened a small store that sold household kitchen and dinner ware, while my grandmother opened three clothing boutiques of her own, each catering to a different sector of the Guatemalan society.

As for the rest of the family in Miami, we began to slowly come to terms with the fact that a return to the Cuba we had known was not to be. We began to settle in our new land and build upon the foundations of our history. By 1967 both my mother and father would become naturalized citizens of the United States, and by association, so would my sister Liz and I. Several of the extended family of aunts and uncles opened their own businesses and made a relatively good living while the children attended school. The *doo-wop* rock and roll teenagers of the extended family who had grown up with the 50's in Cuba were now registering at universities.

The world as well was beginning to also show signs of dramatic changes. In America, Vietnam was still a popular war against world communism, but there were rumblings of a nascent opposition emerging in private conversations that would take a few years to explode into the streets and campuses of the nation. Americans began to also hold the truth of individual freedom as self-evident. All men were in fact created equal, even while they were not always being treated that way. Marches for Civil Rights were taking place in various part of the country as people walked along streets with their arms interlocked forming human chains. On either side of these marchers were often lines of baton-wielding police. Clashes between ordinary people of different ages against a well-armed police force took place frequently. The fact that circumstances had brought us to the south of the United States seem to magnify the sensation that we were bearing witness to an emerging social revolution.

Growing multitudes began to take to the streets in protest against racial discrimination. Martin Luther King was marching in Alabama and Washington, D.C., while people stood for their rights with the simple act of sitting in the front seat of the bus, or demanding to be served at a lunch counter without being rejected because of the color of their skin. The Civil Rights movement was in full bloom while I was growing up in Florida.

http://www.youtube.com/watch?v=yRsX30Jv5nE&feature=related

The Cuban immigrant had been relatively immune to this level of white on black discrimination. We found the level of southern opposition to the black community confusing, especially when National Guard troops were called in to escort school children whose only crime was being black or having a desire for a quality education. Protest and civil disobedience produced crises situations between activists and government authorities. The response of the state and federal governments did nothing but highlight the inequities faced by the African-Americans as the state retaliated with brutal force. The march from Selma, Alabama, to Montgomery on March 7, 1965, was a fifty-four mile protest that was met by state troopers who attacked the marchers with dogs, tear gas and billy clubs, giving rise to such memorable terms as "Bloody Sunday."

Demonstrators in Birmingham, Alabama, are sprayed with high pressure fire hoses with enough pressure to break bones, shocking the nation. [LOOK Collection LOC]

As the newest arrivals to this great land, we were witnessing historical changes taking place all around us, changes that brought fear and wonder at the same time. This was a monumental shift in American society. Individual moral behavior by choice had failed, and the state would soon find itself in the uncomfortable position of having to legislate morality. Still, my life in Florida during those early years was exciting for a child just learning about the world. Life was continuing to present itself as visions and lessons that would shape my view of the world as a man and my interests in politics and the human condition as a whole.

The Cuban tragedy had caused many families to be torn apart, separated by a revolution but united in a common memory of the island left behind. My aunt, Irma Martínez and her husband Antonio Bajuelo had made the heart-wrenching decision to send their son into exile with the first wave of family members without them. Their son Antonio, who carried the childhood nickname "Chíqui", had been sent into exile in 1962 as part of the Cuban Diaspora and was living with his aunt Eliana. The boy had been born with a serious heart defect that required periodic medical attention. As an adolescent in Cuba, he was never allowed to participate in any sporting event that would add strain to his heart. Not to be denied, Chíqui would often sneak out of the house to play baseball with his friends, a concept that I would soon become all too familiar with as well when it came to fishing. Within a few years this young man would simply collapse lifeless in the arms of his cousin.

He was seventeen years old when he died in exile, his parents unable to be at his side. It was a dramatic and tragic day when Irma and Antonio were finally allowed to leave Cuba in 1966 for the United States with the realization that the anticipated reunion with their son would never take place. I recall being present when the first thing his parents asked after gaining freedom was to be driven to the cemetery to see their son's gravesite. It was heartbreaking to bear witness to a father sprawled on the ground containing the remains of his son sobbing uncontrollably. I wished so very much I had been spared that image, but it was not to be.

Meanwhile, Felipe Pazos, Grandfather Carlos's brother-in-law, had been assigned by the Kennedy Administration as a member of the top coordination body of the Alliance for Progress program and was traveling throughout Latin America. This was an aid program for Latin American countries much like the "Marshall Plan" had been for Europe at the end of World War II. The aim of the plan was to assist in the financial development of Latin American countries in an attempt to avoid another revolution like the one in Cuba.

While the family was adjusting to the changing course of direction, America and the world were doing the same. The American community was quickly reaching an emotional and spiritual bottom which would manifest itself in the abandonment of all that the prior generations held of value. It was the beginning of the Age of Aquarius, the emergence of great social change of consciousness that began to spread from two separate fronts of our new land. From the south, the Civil Rights Movement spread north and west, and on the corner of Haight and Ashbury Street in San Francisco, the counterculture movement was being born, beginning its march around the world.

The "Hippie movement"[35] shocked America as it engulfed an entire generation with what was considered to be radical beliefs and alternative lifestyles. Beginning in the United States and spreading across the world, the hippies fueled a movement to expand awareness and stretch norms that had been previously accepted. These were primarily young people between the ages of fifteen and twenty-five, and their protest motto included the slogan never to trust anyone

---

[35] Roger Kimball (October 10, 2013). The Long March: How the Cultural Revolution of the 1960s Changed America. Encounter Books

over thirty. The Cold War had recently shown us how close we could come to self-destruction, just as the mid1960's began to show us how we could self-destruct from within with widespread tensions over growing social issues. This was an awakening experience being felt along generational fault lines, lines that were quickly forming all across America. The society that had opened its doors to us as refugees found itself in a state of continual conflict over the war in Vietnam, race relations, sexual mores, women's rights and the traditions of authority.

The social movement sought revolutionary solutions to the problems of institutionalized American society, testing old norms through the experimentation of new musical sounds, a new appearance, and psychedelic drugs such as LSD and heroin in an attempt to reinterpret the American dream. New cultural forms began to take shape that turned its back on the old consumerism that had permeated our society. Its slogans called for participation in mass protests to institute change or to drop out of society completely.

But the 1960's was also an era of great rejoicing and musical festivals. The Monterey Pop Festival introduced the likes of Jimi Hendrix to America. Our music began to change with the pivotal invasion by the Beatles from England in 1964. The British held their Isle of Wight Festivals that drew big names such as *The Who, The Doors, Joni Mitchell, Bob Dylan* and others. In 1967 Scott McKenzie's rendition of the

Jimi Hendrix at Woodstock
http://www.youtube.com/watch?v=TJ4QF45Vygw&feature=related

song "*San Francisco, Be Sure to Wear Flowers in Your Hair*" brought as many as 100,000 young people from all over the world to celebrate San Francisco's "Summer of Love." And in 1969, while Neil Armstrong was taking his first steps on the moon, tens of thousands were gathering at a farm in upstate New York in what would be called "Woodstock."

Those in control of American government policy began to show the strain from these protest movements. American national and foreign policy began to lose any semblance of common sense as we lost confidence in the decisions of the older generation. Opposition to the Vietnam War, the war that had taken Washington's focus away from Cuba and had killed the "Rafael Plan," began in 1964 on the college campuses of America. The conflict against the Communist world saw American lives being lost in greater numbers in Vietnam. At its peak, over 500 Americans were being killed each week in that foreign war, while their sacrifices were being televised to American households for the very first time in the history of warfare.

As the war escalated, bizarre new rules of engagement were adopted to perpetuate the pain of war and deny complete victory. American forces under attack in Vietnam had to almost request permission to fire back. The enemy could invade from the North Vietnamese territory with impunity, yet our forces had to stay below a demilitarized border. In a particularly bizarre policy, American forces were rewarded based on body count. Strange events began to take place, like artillery shells raining down on cemeteries in order to count the dead bodies a second time. We quickly lost our sense of right and wrong, and our 'can win' attitude came increasingly into question.

No one seemed to know were American society was headed. Large sectors of America's new generation dropped out of society into a state of virtual tribal anarchy. Mass protests against the war further fed the demoralization of our

own troops, as support for their sacrifice eroded and then vanished. Troops would be taunted with such terms as "baby-killers," greeted with revulsion by fellow Americans upon their return from duty, while our government began to distrust its people. President Nixon would personify this distrust by adopting an almost "bunker-like" mentality with a form of paranoia that led him and his staff to formulate an ever growing list of "enemies."

While America changed around us, the family didn't know exactly how to react. The De La Cruz and Martinez clan was aghast at the notion of an entire generation of Americans dropping out of the global war against Communism. Cubans continued to see a world-wide struggle along organized fronts. We interpreted what was happening in America in cold war terms, as the successful infiltration of a sophisticated psychological warfare effort by the Soviet empire on a naïve and susceptibly weak generation. This effort was leading American youth to simply refuse to fight no matter what the cause.

The global struggle against the Communist front was serious business, and it required serious and determined people to stand up to it. I know it sounds like a sound bite now, but we Cubans had been intimately impacted by what to us was a clear and concerted effort by a determined foe to take over the entire world. Our Cuban homeland had been lost, and there was talk of other nations falling like "dominos" throughout the world. And while this growing threat loomed around us, our greatest ally, America, was lying about in dark rooms taking drugs and dancing in the forest. So yes, we were very concerned about the hippie movement and where it was heading.

http://www.youtube.com/watch?v=b97_9YMBebY&feature=related

Inside the comfort and quiet of our home life, my father Eduardo was becoming increasingly successful with Carnation Company, and our situation in life was improving. Eduardo was being considered for a more expanded company role overseas in South America, and in 1967 we received word that Grandfather Carlos Eduardo De La Cruz y Valdéz-Montiél would finally be allowed to leave Havana.

By the late 1960's, Grandfather Carlos had become a frail old man in Cuba, never completely recovering from the loss of his wife six years earlier. His daughter Angelina, my father's sister and my aunt, had remained at his side in order to take care of him as was tradition. Now they were both on their way to freedom.

I remember only images of Grandfather Carlos standing in our Miami home dressed in his customary tropical white suit while he spoke with my father. His visit with us would last only a few days, and no one could have guessed then that this meeting would become our last. In 1968, after seeing both Eduardo in Miami and his first-born Carlos in Alabama, and after settling with family members who had called Puerto Rico their home, Carlos Eduardo De La Cruz y Valdéz-Montiél passed away of a stroke at the age of seventy-nine. My parents, sister and I would be living in our new South American home when news would arrive of his passing. As usual, in keeping with my father's wishes, we do not know exactly when he passed away, or where his burial site is located. Perhaps someday, a future De La Cruz will find him and re-inter him in the Havana he loved next to his wife

Bárbara at the family mausoleum. Unfortunately, that task will have to wait for a future generation.

Chapter Eight

America Struggles: A Change in Course

Have no fear of moving into the unknown. Simply step out fearlessly knowing that I am with you, therefore no harm can befall you; all is very, very well. Do this in complete faith and confidence. We keep moving forward, opening new doors, and doing new things, because we're curious and curiosity keeps leading us down new paths.

<u>Pope John Paul II</u>

The people sat comfortably inside an airplane cabin in mid-flight. I was seated next to the window, with my sister alongside me staring out the cabin window while my mother and father seated across the aisle next to us. It was 1967, and Eduardo had come home with the news that the firm was sending the family to the company operations in Lima, Peru. Seven years after our arrival in the United States, we were once again shifting locations to a new nation. It was an eerie feeling when I suddenly realized we did not have a permanent place to call home. Cuba was no longer an option, and Florida, at least to my parents, was as temporary a location as any other. No one knew, nor did anyone expect we would ever return to Florida again.

As a child, moving yet again to a foreign country was difficult for me. Change, no matter how exciting it might be in the long run, is always in conflict with the narrow vision life places on the inexperienced. Making new friends and creating new fields of play seemed hard and unattainable. My immediate neighborhood, the houses and people I knew, were of great value to me. My world was momentarily shaken when my parents told me we were to move to South America. You might as well have said we were on our way to the moon.

My father turned over the house by the lake to Tony deAngelo, the husband of my mother's cousin Elisa who had met us at the airport the day we defected from Cuba. To make it legal, Eduardo "sold" the home to Tony for one dollar while Tony assumed the payments to the bank. The transaction completed, we left the United States for South America. So the grand plan of life had once again set the family in motion, and despite my resistance to the idea of leaving my friends and school behind, we were on our way.

We flew in a Pan American 707 "clipper ship" aircraft on a direct flight from Miami to the ancient city of Lima, the capital of Peru. This had been my first flight since leaving Cuba into exile, certainly the first flight I could remember. The last thirty minutes of the journey was greeted by a fog-covered coastline below, a seemingly impenetrable carpet of white clouds with the occasional majestic and snow-covered peaks of the great Andes Mountain range piercing into view. These pillars of snow and solid rock seemed to poke out of the clouds like stern sentries, and I wasn't sure if we were being welcomed or suspiciously observed. Suffice to say they were

Peruvian Andes

unnerving, and the sense of unease stayed with me for much of the remaining flight. My fears were magnified when the pilot came over the cabin speakers to state that the aircraft radar system had malfunctioned and that we would be descending blind into the clouds and protruding snow capped mountains in an attempt to land at Lima's international airport. If I recall correctly, the pilot's exact words ended with the phrase, *"we're just going to go down and see what happens."* Great, I thought, so what better way to relieve the stress than to start one last fight with my sister Liz while my mother held on to a statue of Santa Bárbara against her chest and prayed.

Our destination was full of mystery for me yet I was resistant and apprehensive, if not unconvinced. We arrived in the coastal capital of Lima, welcomed by the foggy weather which dwells around the city for the most part of the year. Legend says that the grounds of Lima were once an Indian cemetery, pointed out to the conquering Spaniards as the best location for their capital in the hope that the dead would avenge the crimes committed on the indigenous people. Be that as it may, the grey skies and gloomy days of Lima gave the city a mystical aura of antiquity and beauty.

The Capital is the largest city of Peru, located on the coast overlooking the Pacific Ocean. The place had been conquered by the Spanish conquistador Francisco Pizarro as far back as 1535, and it remained one of the most important cities in the Spanish viceroyalty of Peru, so I was intrigued. The City itself was usually covered by a cold, damp mist, which the people there called the 'Garúa,' giving the place an almost magical feel. Historic Lima is an enchanting haven of a period long gone, and it would for the next five years become my home.

The Cathedral in the Main Plaza of Lima

The cultural rebellion in America was just reaching maturity when the immediate De La Cruz family moved to South America, so we were somewhat immune to the full brunt of the changes that were taking place in the first world. While we moved far away from what was occurring in the United States, we were not completely oblivious to its impact or its consequences. The kind of clash that was occurring in

America was also taking place all over the world. Peru also felt those same ripples, but the nation continued to reside in an almost unique and different era and time.

    We had moved away from the United States, a country where time is of the essence and no one seemed to have enough of it. By contrast, Peru was a nation with a striking contrast of slow, calculated movements for everyday life in the late 60's. The local population had a term for it; they called it "the enhancement of Joy." The mornings woke with the sounds of street vendors in our suburban neighborhoods slowly pulling their carts along the way while attempting to sell fresh bread. Another would sell fresh vegetables, while still another carried brooms and kitchen wares. This was not a region of supermarkets as in the United States; this was a place where the markets seemed to make house calls and time made every effort to stand still.

    We lived in a land that demanded its people to contemplate, reflect and observe their everyday surroundings. An almost spiritual people, Peruvians demonstrated little sense of stress or pressure that I could observe. We began our day so completely different from what we were used to in America; the mornings were essentially quiet, interrupted only by the occasional sound of doves flying in with the cool Pacific breeze. In a significant way we did leave the cultural changes of America behind. This was a land that was far away from the epicenter of the now world-wide social clashes, and it was perhaps that which gave it its greatest appeal.

The social upheaval in America peaked around 1968-1970. The year 1968 in particular was a world historical year. We had in 1968 the Vietnamese Tet offensive, when North Vietnamese troops launched their most serious and heaviest attack on American forces in Vietnam. Every major American military base was simultaneously attacked in a surprise offensive. Enemy forces managed to even penetrate the American Embassy in Saigon, and a firefight ensued on Embassy grounds.

Although the North Vietnamese suffered heavy losses, it set off a world-wide dynamic. Throughout the world there was a sense of chaos. I truly believed in 1968 that we had reached a critical point in our global society, and I wasn't sure civilization would survive it. In Czechoslovakia a nonviolent rebellion against Soviet domination called the "Prague Spring" led to an invasion of half a million Soviet troops. In France student uprisings called the "May events"[36] caused mass public strikes, shutting down two-thirds of the country and sparking similar movements in Spain, Senegal, Italy and

---

[36] Touraine, Alain. <u>The May Movement: Revolt and Reform</u>

Mexico City, where students rose up in solidarity with the French. Hundreds of students were killed in Mexico City by Mexican police and troops.

The Mexican incident occurred just before the opening of the 1968 Summer Olympics, where we witnessed American athletes who had won the gold and silver medals raising their fists in a sign of Black power, as a symbol more important than national pride. Something cynical and diabolical was hovering over all nations in 1968, killing our leaders and radicalizing our young, while the Soviet Empire still sought our annihilation and nuclear war was still a very real possibility.

Outside a drab, two-story motor inn on Mulberry Street in downtown Memphis, a man took position with a weapon in hand. The sign outside identified it as the Lorraine Motel in Memphis, Tennessee. It was 6:00 p.m. on the 4th of April, as the man took aim through the scope of a high-powered rifle. His target came into view as the Reverend Martin Luther King, Jr. standing on the balcony just outside of Room number 306. At 6:01 p.m. the rifle launched its message of hate and death, taking the life of this non-violent man.[37]

---

[37] Dyson, Michael Eric (2008). "Fighting Death". April 4, 1968: Martin Luther King Jr.'s death and how it changed America. New York: Basic Civitas Books

Martin Luther King had spent thirteen years of this life dedicated to peaceful protest against social injustice. He had become the promise of millions and had been awarded the 1964 Nobel Prize for Peace. Now, he lay sprawled on the balcony's floor, felled by a sniper's bullet. Within fifteen minutes of the shot, Martin Luther King arrived at St. Joseph's Hospital on a stretcher with an oxygen mask over his face. He had been hit by a .30-06 caliber rifle bullet that had entered his right jaw and then traveled through his neck, severing his spinal cord. Martin Luther King, Jr. would be pronounced dead at 7:05p.m. He was thirty-nine. An escaped convict, James Earl Ray would be captured two months later while trying to leave the United Kingdom on a false Canadian passport in the name of Ramón George Sneyd on his way to white-ruled Rhodesia.

The leader of the American Civil Rights Movement had formed a key element in the larger counterculture movement. I recall waiting at our Miraflores neighborhood with several other children for the school bus to take us to the private American School in Lima, when a car driven by the wife of the American Counsel in Lima suddenly stopped in front of us. Frantically lowering her window, she hurriedly blurted out to her son Steven who was at my side that she was on her way to the American Embassy, having heard of the assassination of Martin Luther King, Jr. It was April 4th, 1968.

Such was the course direction of 1968. King's assassination led to riots and destruction in over 150 cities throughout the United States. More damage was done to the city of Washington, D.C. during these riots than was done during the war of 1812 when the British burned down the White House. To further add to the chaos of that year, the

Sniper fire kills Reverend Martin Luther King Jr.
http://www.youtube.com/watch?v=cmOBbxgxKvo

Pentagon concluded in 1968 that it did not have enough troops to fight the war in Vietnam and maintain order at home. The world seemed to be coming undone, out of control.

That same year, a large gathering of people were in a banquet room of a hotel united in celebration. A rather young-looking politician was completing a victory speech from the dais, adjusting his hair and giving the crowd a victory sign with his hand. The crowd gathered in the large ballroom responded with cheers and praises at a man in the podium. It was June of 1968, and Bobby Kennedy, the man who had held so much influence over Grandfather Rafael's Mambise Commandos and the CIA effort to depose Fidel Castro, had just won the California primary elections for the nomination to run as the presidential candidate for the Democratic Party of the United States. It was just after midnight on June 5th in Los Angeles's Ambassador Hotel. There had been a change in plans after the speech. Kennedy was supposed to walk through the open ballroom to meet with other supporters, but time would not allow it, and instead he was rushed through the kitchen pantry of the hotel, the prey to the hunter.

    Kennedy and his aides started down a passageway narrowed by an ice machine against the right wall and a steam table to the left. As Robert Kennedy turned to his left to shake hands with a busboy named Juan Romero, when Sirhan Sirhan, a Christian-born Palestinian stepped down from a low tray-stacker beside the ice machine, rushed past Kennedy's aid and repeatedly fired a .22 caliber Iver-Johnson Cadet revolver at the candidate's head. The assassin's weapon met its mark and history was once again fulfilled.[38]

---

[38] Dooley, Brian (1996). Robert Kennedy: The Final Years. New York: St. Martin's

Sirhan was motivated by Middle Eastern politics and the support America had given to the state of Israel. That would be the simple answer, but I believed he was also an early point man in the coming wave that would engulf and

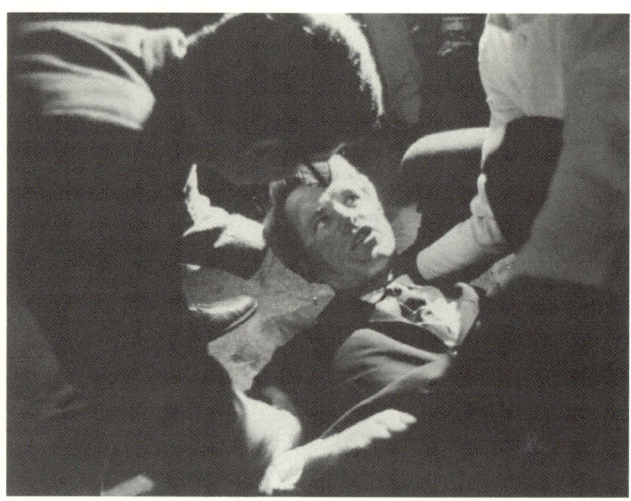

Bobby Kennedy lays mortally wounded after being shot in 1968
http://www.youtube.com/watch?v=lmc2EzkRDkI

preoccupy humanity for decades to come. This was the beginning of the world-wide transition from political to religious fanaticism, and it would clash with humanity with a force that resembled something Biblical, like the second horseman of the apocalypse that I had sensed for years was on its way. The change was subtle, almost subliminal. The shift from the political to the religious justification for violence first showed up as a mixture of both. To the western world and the family, it would clarify itself further as Islamic fundamentalism and it would have a direct impact on the future of our adopted nation.

We had been living for decades under the onslaught of political fanatics that were bent on destroying our civilization. That movement had seen its peak with the Cuban Missile Crisis and its failure to destroy the world. That first horseman of the apocalypse would finally succumb with the fall of the Soviet Empire in 1989, replaced by a new horseman that was slowly beginning its gallop. Even at that young age in 1968-1970, I felt a shift to a new strategy of evil, a new world force that was just now at its infancy.

The Arab, Palestinian, Israeli conflict was the match that lit the fuse, with the fate of Jerusalem as its ultimate prize. It inherently began as a political dispute that brought on several wars. It was now moving into the domain of religious radicalism, and it would be this battle that would guide the history of the world for the balance of the twentieth century and the beginning of the twenty-first. This new wave of Islamic fundamentalism would have a direct impact on the De La Cruz family and with me as well as my future wife in particular.

No one event began the downward social and public order spiral. It was just one of those moments in world history where all the various forces that shape mankind seemed to coalesce and intersect. The movement and the resulting disturbances and violence didn't begin or end on a strict calendar time. The sixties themselves didn't get started until at least 1963, and the psychodrama of 1968 arguably opened with the death of Che Guevara in the fall of 1967.

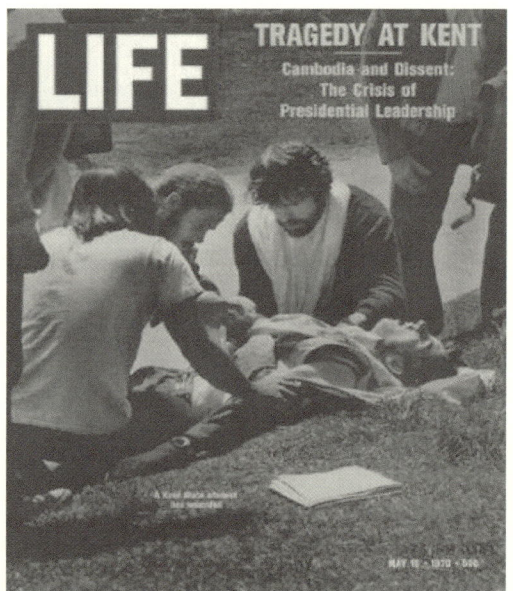

American troops fire on university students at Kent Sate
http://www.youtube.com/watch?v=KW5tJ4_-9uE&feature=related

After the Cuban revolution was consolidated, the Argentinian Che Guevara ventured out into other parts of the world to spread revolution. He had been in the Congo in Africa and in Central America. In 1967, while attempting to overthrow the Bolivian government with a band of rebels, the army as well as Cuban exiles on station with the CIA, located and captured him. Shortly after his capture, he was executed by firing squad before he could become an even larger symbol for the revolutionary circles.

It is ironic to me that Che Guevara, who did so much to destroy capitalism, is now a quintessential capitalist brand. His likeness adorns T-shirts, mugs, baseball caps and various other items with his picture taken by photographer Alberto Korda.

It seemed funny to me how life takes on its own course. Che is now big corporate business. In Havana, Guevara murdered or oversaw the executions in summary trials of scores of people—proven enemies, suspected enemies, and those who happened to be in the wrong place at the wrong time. According to the testimony of Jaime Costa Vázquez, a former commander in the revolutionary army known as "El Catalán," Che's standing instruction was *"If in doubt, kill him."*[39] Guevara was a callous fool.

While Che left written testimony of his cruelties, his early death meant that he did not live to take full responsibility for Cuba's hell. Myth can tell you as much about an era as truth. Thanks to Che's own written testimonials to his thoughts and his deeds, we may know exactly how deluded so many of our contemporaries are about so much.

The turmoil of 1968 marched on while the family moved forward. That same year, more than 10,000 people gathered in Philadelphia in response to the Black Panther party's call to write a new constitution for the United States. This new document was to be *internationalist*; it called for the abolition of a standing army to be replaced by popular militias, complete liberation for women, and for communal spaces to be set aside for children to be free. In response to all these events, there was massive police presence in an attempt to bring the demonstrations under some semblance of control.

My family, indeed, the overwhelming majority of the people did not know how to proceed further. The society had come to a halt and there was no socially legitimate faction that could lead the people forward. In 1970 there were the killings

---

[39] Che Guevara, Murderer. August 3, 2005 by Richard Nikoley

at Kent State and Jackson State Universities, resulting in a strike of four million students and faculty, the largest strike in the history of the United States. I was five years away from attending the University of California in Los Angeles (UCLA) through a Naval ROTC program in 1970. During that year, the ROTC office that I would call home for four years of university study was destroyed by a bomb.

My personal response or reaction to this counter-culture movement was fear. Part of me was attracted to the ideals of the movement, but part of me still didn't get it; not then. As I look back now, I realize that what we were witnessing was not the total abandonment of what we held as truths, but in a large extent, a reaffirmation of it. This was not a planned psychological assault from the evil Soviet Empire, but an almost spiritual rebirth of our nation, an awakening that led to a healthier, more mature society. We had been living for decades in a world we viewed in a narrow scope of black and white, never stopping to consider the possibility that there may be an alternative view of life and the world that might actually bring in some color to our lives. I realized that my fears stemmed from the reaction to how the older generation was responding to the movement. Certainly this movement was strange, but it yearned to be guided, if not embraced. I believe we emerged stronger as a people, shed the incessant need to attain the material and began to see each other as brothers and sisters.

What I feared back then would decades later be replaced by a fear of returning to the days prior to the 1960 and 1970's movement. I see today a generation that is more concerned with self-importance and material wealth, ignorant of all that had been achieved on their behalf during the 60's. The movement had planted a seed of change that lasted longer than the psychedelic look and the unkempt appearance of its members. Eventually the hippie movement grew older and moderated their lives and their views, and especially after US involvement in the Vietnam War ended in the mid-1970s, the counter-culture was largely absorbed by the mainstream, leaving a lasting impact on philosophy, morality, music, art, lifestyle and fashion that continues even today. There was a cultural shift that led to greater freedoms for people who are different or perceived to be different.

The conflicts of the Civil Rights and the Hippie Movements were classic irresistible forces meeting up with the immovable object of social custom and an archaic perception of the world. But with time and perseverance, the movement succeeded in forcing a collective look inside ourselves. This had been a war where we had achieved total victory, making the necessary changes to reaffirm our humanity. And even as we felt an increasing confidence that we would survive the turmoil's confronting us at the height of the Cold War and the social revolutions, we felt the loss of what we had left behind. The future was still unclear, but we understood it to be ours to make of it what we desired. Generations of my family had worked hard to build and adjust to whatever life had decided to throw their way. We had not only taken up the challenge, but we endeavored to change and mold it into something more understandable, something that we could look back years later and feel a sense of pride. I understood clearly at this turning point in our history, that it would soon be my turn, and those that would come after me, to finish the twentieth century and enter the twenty-first with the responsibility to somehow improve on where my fathers and grandfathers had left off.

Book 4: **_"Echoes of Our Sons"_** to follow

Bibliography

1. Piero Gleijeses: "Cuba's First Venture in Africa: Algeria, 1961–1965". Journal of Latin American Studies 28 (1). 1996.

2. Review: Perception and Paradox in the Cold War. Vol. 21, No. 3 (Sep., 1993), Published by: Johns Hopkins University Press

3. Powers, Francis (2004). Operation Overflight. 22841 Quicksilver Drive Dulles, Virginia 20166: Brassey's, INC.

4. Watry, David M. Diplomacy at the Brink: Eisenhower, Churchill, and Eden in the Cold War. Baton Rouge: Louisiana State University Press, 2014.

5. Bissell, Richard M. Jr., with Jonathan E. Lewis and Frances T. Pudlo. Reflections of a Cold Warrior: From Yalta to the Bay of Pigs (New Haven and London: Yale University Press, 1996

6. Coltman, Leycester (2003). The Real Fidel Castro. New Haven and London: Yale University Press.

7. Inside the Cuban Revolution: Fidel Castro and the Urban Underground. By Julia Sweig

8. Michael Grow. "Cuba, 1961". U.S. Presidents and Latin American Interventions: Pursuing Regime Change in the Cold War. Lawrence: University of Kansas Press, 2008.

9. Jack Anderson (1971-01-18). "6 Attempts to Kill Castro Laid to CIA". The Washington Post.

10. Lamar Waldron and Thom Hartmann (2005). Ultimate Sacrifice: John and Robert Kennedy, the Plan for a Coup in Cuba, and the Murder of JFK. New York: Carroll & Graf Publishers.

11. Ted Shackley and Richard A. Finney (1992). Spymaster: my life in the CIA. Dulles, Virginia: Potomac Books, Inc..

12. Campbell, Duncan (April 3, 2006). "638 ways to kill Castro". London: The Guardian Unlimited. Retrieved 2006-05-28.

13. Bohning, Don (2005). The Castro Obsession: U.S. Covert Operations Against Cuba, 1959–1965. Washington, D.C.: Potomac Books, Inc.

14. Pfeiffer, Jack B. 1979. Official History of the Bay of Pigs Operation, Vol.I Air Operations, Part 1

15. Pfeiffer, Jack B. 1979. Official History of the Bay of Pigs Operation, Vol.I Air Operations, Part 2

16. de Quesada, Alejandro; Walsh, Stephen. 2009. The Bay of Pigs: Cuba 1961. Osprey Elite series

17. Schlesinger, Arthur M. Jr. 1965, 2002. A Thousand Days: John F. Kennedy in the White House. Houghton Mifflin

18. Pedlow, Gregory W. and Donald E. Welzenbach. The Central Intelligence Agency and Overhead Reconnaissance: The U-2 and OXCART Programs, 1954-1974. Washington, DC: Central Intelligence Agency, 1992.

19. McGeorge Bundy, Memorandum of Meeting with President Kennedy, White House, Washington, February 8, 1961

20. Scheman, L. Ronald (1988). The Alliance for Progress: A Retrospective. New York:

21. The Very Best Men: Four Who Dared: The Early Years of the CIA. By Evan Thomas (Author)

22. Hedegaard, Erik (April 5, 2007). "The Last Confessions of E. Howard Hunt". Rolling Stone. Archived from the original on June 18, 2008.

23. A Guide to the Rafael Martínez Pupo Papers Relating to Comandos Mambises. Finding aid created by Margarita Vargas-Betancourt. University of Florida Smathers Libraries - Special and Area Studies Collections. November 2011

24. One Minute to Midnight: Kennedy, Khrushchev, and Castro on the Brink of Nuclear War Paperback – June 2, 2009 by Michael Dobbs

25. Mindsets and Missiles: A Firsthand Account of the Cuban Missile Crisis. By Kenneth Michael Absher

26. Deadly Secrets (Thunders Mouth Press, NY 1992) William Turner and Warren Hinckle

27. Hunt, E. Howard. 1973. Give Us This Day. Arlington House, New Rochelle, NY.

28. Carr, Raymond, and Fusi, Juan Pablo. 1991 (1979). Spain: Dictatorship to democracy. London: Routledge.

29. How Cuba aided revolutionary Algeria in 1963 – themilitant.com

30. Heggoy, A.A. (1970), "Colonial origins of the Algerian-Moroccan border conflict of October 1963", African Studies Review

31. Harrison, Alexander (1989). Challenging De Gaulle: The OAS and the counterrevolution in Algeria (1954-1962). Greenwood press

32. Diamond, Robert (1970). France under De Gaulle. Facts on File

33. Jackson, Gabriel (1965). The Spanish Republic and the Civil War, 1931–1939. Princeton: Princeton University Press.

34. Payne, Stanley G. (2004). The Spanish Civil War, the Soviet Union, and Communism. New Haven; London: Yale University Press.

35. Barkaoui, Miloud. "Kennedy and the Cold War imbroglio - the case of Algeria's independence." Arab Studies Quarterly. Spring 1999

36. The Brilliant Disaster: JFK, Castro, and America's Doomed Invasion of Cuba's By Jim Rasenberger

37. 40 Years After Missile Crisis, Players Swap Stories in Cuba. By Kevin Sullivan, Washington Post Foreign Service.Sunday, October 13, 2002

38. "Cuban Missile Crisis, 1962: A Political Perspective after 40 Years," National Security Archive. Created and maintained by George Washington University, Washington, D.C.

39. Dyson, Michael Eric (2008). "Fighting Death". April 4, 1968: Martin Luther King Jr.'s death and how it changed America. New York: Basic Civitas Books.

40. Dooley, Brian (1996). Robert Kennedy: The Final Years. New York: St. Martin's.

41. Branch, Taylor. At Canaan's Edge: America In the King Years, 1965–1968. New York: Simon & Schuster, 2006.

42. Smith, Peter H (1999). Talons of the Eagle: Dynamics of U.S.-Latin American Relations. Oxford University Press.

43. Smith, Tony "The Alliance for Progress: The 1960s,"

44. Roger Kimball (October 10, 2013). The Long March: How the Cultural Revolution of the 1960s Changed America. Encounter Books.

45. Gail Dolgin; Vicente Franco (2007). American Experience: The Summer of Love. PBS. Retrieved April 23, 2007.

46. Perry, Charles (2005), The Haight-Ashbury: A History (Reprint ed.), Wenner Books,

47. Touraine, Alain. The May Movement: Revolt and Reform

48. Che Guevara, Murderer. August 3, 2005 by Richard Nikoley

49. Gangsterismo: The United States, Cuba, and the Mafia, 1933-1966) by Jack Colhoun -

50. The Black Panther Ten-Point Program". The North American Review 253 (4): 16–17. July–August 1968.